CONTENTS

1218843

CONTENTS

THE ROMANCE OF THE BEAVER

Printed in England.

THE ROMANCE
OF THE BEAVER

Being the History of the Beaver in the Western Hemisphere.

By A. RADCLYFFE DUGMORE

F.R.G.S., F.R.C.S.

ILLUSTRATED WITH PHOTOGRAPHS FROM
LIFE AND DRAWINGS BY THE AUTHOR

> Should you ask where Nawadaha
> Found these songs, so wild and wayward,
> Found these legends and traditions,
> I should answer, I should tell you,
> " In the birds'-nests of the forest,
> In the lodges of the beaver."
>
> *The Song of Hiawatha.*

PHILADELPHIA :
J. B. LIPPINCOTT COMPANY
LONDON : WILLIAM HEINEMANN

THE ROMANCE OF THE PRAYER

THE ROMANCE OF THE BEAVER

Silently sank Pau-Puk-Keewis;
Black became his shirt of deerskin,
Black his moccasins and leggings,
In a broad black tail behind him
Spread his fox-tails and his fringes;
He was changed into a beaver.
    'Make me large,' said Pau-Puk-
    Keewis,
'Make me large and make me
    larger,
Larger than the other beavers.'
'Yes,' the beaver chief responded,
'When our lodge below you enter,
In our wigwam we will make you
Ten times larger than the others.'
    Thus into the clear brown water
Silently sank Pau-Puk-Keewis:
Found the bottom covered over
With the trunks of trees and
    branches,
Hoards of food against the winter,
Piles and heaps against the famine;
Found the lodge with arching door-
    way,
Leading into spacious chambers.
    Here they made him large and
    larger,
Made him largest of the beavers,
Ten times larger than the others.
'You shall be our ruler,' said they;
'Chief and King of all the beavers.'
    But not long had Pau - Puk -
    Keewis
Sat in state among the beavers,
When there came a voice of warn-
    ing
From the watchman at his station
In the water-flags and lilies,
Saying, 'Here is Hiawatha!
Hiawatha with his hunters!'
    Then they heard a cry above
    them,

Heard a shouting and a tramping,
Heard a crashing and a rushing,
And the water round and o'er
    them
Sank and sucked away in eddies,
And they knew their dam was
    broken.
    On the lodge's roof the hunters
Leaped, and broke it all asunder;
Streamed the sunshine through the
    crevice,
Sprang the beavers through the
    doorway,
Hid themselves in deeper water,
In the channel of the streamlet;
But the mighty Pau-Puk-Keewis
Could not pass beneath the door-
    way;
He was puffed with pride and
    feeding,
He was swollen like a bladder.
    Through the roof looked Hia-
    watha,
Cried aloud, 'O Pau-Puk-Keewis!
Vain are all your craft and cun-
    ning,
Vain your manifold disguises!
Well I know you, Pau-Puk-Keewis!'
    With their clubs they beat and
    bruised him,
Beat to death poor Pau - Puk -
    Keewis,
Pounded him as maize is pounded,
Till his skull was crushed to pieces.
    Six tall hunters, lithe and limber,
Bore him home on poles and
    branches,
Bore the body of the beaver;
But the ghost, the Jeebi in him,
Thought and felt as Pau - Puk -
    Keewis,
Still lived on as Pau-Puk-Keewis.

From The Song of Hiawatha.

Through bush, and brake, and forest,
Ran the cunning Pau-Puk-Keewis;
Like an antelope he bounded,
Till he came unto a streamlet
In the middle of the forest,
To a streamlet still and tranquil,
That had overflowed its margin,
To a dam made by the beavers,
To a pond of quiet water,
Where knee-deep the trees were standing,
Where the water-lilies floated,
Where the rushes waved and whispered.
  On the dam stood Pau-Puk-Keewis,
On the dam of trunks and branches,
Through whose chinks the water spouted,
O'er whose summit flowed the streamlet.
From the bottom rose the beaver,
Looked with two great eyes of wonder,
Eyes that seemed to ask a question,
At the stranger, Pau-Puk-Keewis.
  On the dam stood Pau-Puk-Keewis,
O'er his ankles flowed the streamlet,
Flowed the bright and silvery water,
And he spake unto the beaver,
With a smile he spake in this wise:
  'O my friend Ahmeek, the beaver,
Cool and pleasant is the water;
Let me dive into the water,
Let me rest there in your lodges;
Change me, too, into a beaver!'
  Cautiously replied the beaver,
With reserve he thus made answer:

'Let me first consult the others.
Let me ask the other beavers.'
Down he sank into the water,
Heavily sank he, as a stone sinks,
Down among the leaves and branches,
Brown and matted at the bottom.
  On the dam stood Pau-Puk-Keewis,
O'er his ankles flowed the streamlet,
Spouted through the chinks below him,
Dashed upon the stones beneath him,
Spread serene and calm before him;
And the sunshine and the shadows
Fell in flecks and gleams upon him,
Fell in little shining patches,
Through the waving, rustling branches.
  From the bottom rose the beavers,
Silently above the surface
Rose one head and then another,
Till the pond seemed full of beavers,
Full of black and shining faces.
  To the beavers Pau-Puk-Keewis
Spake entreating, said in this wise:
'Very pleasant is your dwelling,
O my friends! and safe from danger;
Can you not with all your cunning,
All your wisdom and contrivance,
Change me, too, into a beaver?'
  'Yes!' replied Ahmeek, the beaver,
He the King of all the beavers,
'Let yourself slide down among us,
Down into the tranquil water.'
  Down into the pond among them

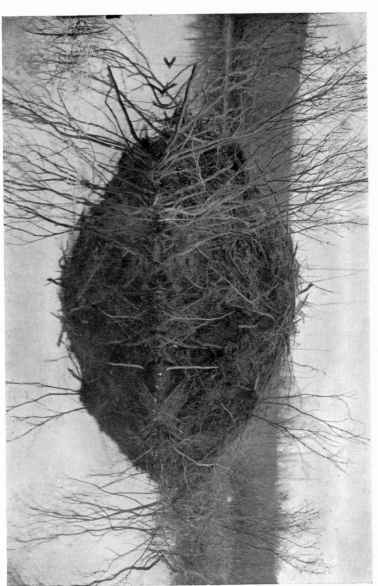

The beaver lodge plastered over with the protective coating of mud, which when frozen renders the inmates safe from any enemies except man.

Beaver in the act of cutting a branch off a lodged birch tree. The flashlight was fired by the beaver.

LIST OF ILLUSTRATIONS

ILLUSTRATIONS IN THE TEXT

DEDICATED

BY

SPECIAL PERMISSION TO

H.R.H.
THE DUKE OF CONNAUGHT,
K.G., K.T., K.P., P.C., ETC.,

GOVERNOR-GENERAL OF CANADA.

INTRODUCTION

THE object of this little book is two-fold : first, as people of nearly all classes and ages appear to be interested in the life and habits of the beaver, to provide a book on the subject free from exaggeration, and not too technical ; secondly, to call attention to the question of protecting the most interesting animal to-day extant. We are apt to drift along so busied by our own affairs that the future is too often forgotten, as indeed is the immediate present, except in so far as it intimately affects us and our daily lives. Occasionally we wake up—some of us at least—and realise with a shock that something is slipping from our grasp, that the world is in imminent danger of losing some particular and interesting form of life, for once a species is gone no power of man will ever recall it. If our awakening is not too late, and our energies are sufficient, we make a great cry that is heard far and near and the species is perhaps saved. If our cry is only half-hearted, the disappearance of the bird or animal is arrested, and we are satisfied ; but apathy follows only too often, and then more than likely

R.B.   B

the destruction continues, and at our second awakening we are probably too late.

We owe a great deal to those who follow us, for we are the stewards into whose keeping the world is entrusted; we populate the world with our children who have the right to ask an account of our stewardship, and their children, and their children's children after them. As we build museums and libraries to store away and preserve to the best of our ability those things which though perishable, we believe to be of interest, so must we do all in our power to protect the birds and animals that are practically imperishable except through man's too frequent destructive agency. Some animals are probably doomed to extermination, as wild creatures at any rate, and perhaps also as captives; among these are the lions, leopards, rhino-ceroses and others, whose methods of life are not conducive to human advancement and comfort. They can only be preserved as mounted specimens and in photographs; such pictures whether single or cinematographs will be of untold interest to those who follow us and we should feel the obliga-tion of not only securing really good negatives but of having those we have got properly cared for. Too often have I urged this and yet how little is being done! With the beaver it is not so much a question of securing photographs, for the beaver do not lend themselves to pictorial efforts. It is a question of securing for him proper protection.

What Colonel Roosevelt, Dr. W. T. Hornaday (of the New York Zoological Society), the Audubon Societies, the Museum of Natural History of New York and other organisations and individuals have done for birds, and some animals, should be done for the beaver. The perpetuation of the species could be carried on with so little trouble, and the results would repay the efforts ten-thousandfold.

If this little book does anything to call attention to the question of adequate protection either in the United States, Canada, Newfoundland, and elsewhere, the many years of hard work will be more than amply repaid. In treating the subject I have avoided all mention of methods of trapping as it is intended as a constructive and not a destructive work. Someone will come after me who will no doubt treat the subject of beaver life far better and with greater thoroughness. That work will, I trust, be received with gratitude. In the meantime those who are interested in the subject will perhaps experience some slight pleasure from this effort to call attention to the beaver, his work, and its far-reaching effects.

Among those to whom I am indebted for information are many who have passed to the land of shadows, but have left behind them the results of their observations. I therefore offer my thanks, both to the living and the dead—most conspicuous among them being Lewis H. Morgan, for "The

American Beaver and His Works" (published in
1868 by J. B. Lippincott & Co.), Horace T. Martin, F.Z.S., &c., for "Castorologia, or the History
and Traditions of the Canadian Beaver" (1892),
Ernest Thompson Seton for "Life Histories of
Northern Animals," and Enos A. Mills for "In
Beaver World" (1913), and to the Jesuit fathers.

For the photographs which illustrate this volume
I can but say that I have done my best, and have
never spared myself in my efforts to get the most
satisfactory results. Some of the photographs of
the animals themselves have been slightly re-
touched. It is my first offence in this direction,
and has only been done because after careful consideration it seemed so very necessary. The reader
will never realise the amount of labour that has
been devoted to securing the pictures given, for
they are illustrations rather than pictures. Let
him therefore pass over their defects with a kindly
consideration and not be too severe if in the text
he finds statements which do not agree with his
own ideas and experiences.

A. RADCLYFFE DUGMORE.

CRETE HILL,
    SOUTH NUTFIELD.

CHAPTER 1

THE BEAVERS OF NORTH AMERICA. THEIR HABITS OF LIFE AND THEIR WONDERFUL ENGINEERING FEATS

IN a quiet pond, far away in the wilds of Canada, a small, dark object appeared silently and without disturbing the serenity of the placid waters. A few minutes later, the small object moved slowly along, and lengthening quivering lines made the inverted images of the opposite trees tremble in the reflected sunset so that the dark greens of the firs and rich reds and yellows of the birches and maples danced together in the ripples. The dark object was a beaver and he was filled with the fear of man, inherited through a long line of ancestors who had striven to outwit those that sought their destruction. This survivor of a much persecuted race had sought the far away country with the hope of being able to live with his family unmolested by the constant dread of the steel trap. Unlimited care and constant watchfulness were the price he must be always ready to pay for his safety. And even so the chances were entirely against him.

Not until the sun had set, and the sky was lighted by the glorious afterglow, had he ventured to leave the protection of his well-built house. A long swim under water brought him to the middle of the pond which he and his family had made. From this point he could inspect the encircling hillsides, and the friendly currents of air would perhaps carry to his keen nose the scent of any human enemy who might be lurking in the neighbourhood. Apparently the evening breeze was untainted by man-scent. But the beaver considered it wise to make still more sure, so he swam a short distance, and then disappeared beneath the water so softly that scarcely a ripple marked the place where he had dived. A few minutes later, he quietly reappeared close to the shore on the lee side of the pond. Once more he remained as still as a floating log, his nose pointed toward the almost imperceptible breeze, his dark rounded ears raised to catch the slightest sound. Then slowly and silently he swam round the pond closely following the irregular shore line. No sign of danger could he find. Evidently no stranger had come near his home since he had entered his house that morning. So when he came to where the water was very shallow he cut off a small willow branch and proceeded to nibble the bark for his supper.

In the stillness of the evening the grating sound of his sharp teeth cutting through the bark sounded loudly. His family in the lodge at the further end of the pond heard it and knew that they could

Beaver swimming.

A large birch tree cut by the beavers and dropped into the water. All the
branches are to be cut and carried away, while the trunk, which is too
thick to be conveniently cut, is being stripped of its bark for the
immediate needs of the animals.

come forth with safety. Three small heads soon appeared on the surface of the water near the house and soon another and larger one. She was the mother of the three, and she was satisfied that her husband had sufficiently well examined the immediate vicinity. So without wasting time she and her youngsters proceeded each to their particular choice of shrub or tree and ate what they wanted.

It was in the month of October, the busiest month in the beavers' year. The cold nights warned them of the approaching winter. The glistening white frost which covered the grass each night with its myriad crystals and the thin sheets of " window-pane " ice which bordered the pond were the forerunners of the cold that would come later. The terrible, relentless cold which held all that northern country in its icy embrace, which made the ponds resemble solid land and subdued the most turbulent streams by converting them into irregular masses of snow-covered ice ; the cold which so often for months at a time held the beavers prisoners in their houses, free only to roam in the pond beneath the shadow of the impenetrable ice ; the pitiless cold which spreads famine among the dwellers of the northern woods so that hunger-bred courage, and the cunning persistence which comes from necessity, renders the wolves and gluttons a source of danger to all beavers, especially to those who are not well-housed. Therefore, in

October or even earlier, the beavers must work diligently and make use of the extraordinary intelligence which they have developed through the thousands of years since they became as we know them to-day.

The beavers we have been watching in the little far-away pond spent but a short time over their afternoon tea. The time for enjoyment and ease had passed, and they must get to work. The dam had to be finished. The house needed its outside coating of mud and there was still a large amount of wood to be cut for the winter supply. Altogether an appalling lot to be done in the short time that remained before winter; and so the little animals left their partly-peeled twigs and each went to do that which he considered most necessary for the welfare of the family. The father first made a careful inspection of the dam and found many places which were in need of additional material. This he procured from the bottom of the pond, bringing up big sods of earth and partly decayed grass which he carried in his hands, under his chin. As these were brought to the dam he pushed them into position, arranging every piece so that the structure was level and fairly smooth. Here and there a stick or short log was deemed necessary; some of these he found on the water's edge, others on the shore. The mother beaver in the meantime was busily engaged in improving the house. This needed more sticks and the weak places had to be filled in with sod and mud. The young assisted in this work, each bringing his small load and arranging it as he had seen his parents do. Occasionally, the family stopped work altogether and took time to nibble a little bark from some particularly tempting branch. Then a very important work demanded attention. The cutting of trees and gathering of the winter supply of food. On this must depend their safety during the cold weather. A few days ago, they had felled a large birch tree which had dropped on the edge of the pond. Already they had cut off many of the most accessible branches and now they continued the work of stripping the trunk of its limbs. Some were so large that it was necessary to cut them into several sections, their length depending on the thickness. As each piece was cut through with their keen-edged teeth, it was floated across the water to the pile near the house. In swimming, the beaver held the branch with his teeth, and on arriving at the food pile, he would take a fresh grip with his teeth and dive down carrying the branch with him. Then the whole pile would tremble slightly as he forced the piece into the tangled mass of sticks, well below the surface of the water. Trip after trip was made in this manner, each trip adding its mite to the great supply of winter food, and while the young were thus engaged one of the old ones was up in the woods searching for a fresh tree to cut down.

Many things had to be considered in the selection of a suitable tree. It must be in a place where it could be easily cut, and not too far from the water. Then it should be clear of other trees so that it would fall—unfortunately they often make mistakes in this respect—and finally what is of great importance, the tree must be in the right condition. That could only be ascertained by cutting into the bark, and as he went about he marked several trees in this way before finding one that suited his fastidious taste. Then, sitting on his hind legs, with his large, heavy tail as a balance, he commenced the hard work of biting through the tough wood, after first eating the coating of bark. The noise made by his sharp teeth tearing out the great chips sounded loud in the still evening. Crunch, crunch, crunch, crunch, then a pause as he dropped the clean cut chips; and again the crunching resounded through the darkening woods. For half an hour this continued. Then as a beaver does not like to work too long on any one task, he shuffled off, leaving the birch tree with its gaping wound gleaming white against the sombre background.

There was a road to make from where that tree would fall, down to the pond, so the beaver attended to that, combining pleasure with his labours, for as he found small saplings of hazel or mountain ash growing in the line of the path, he cut them down and ate off some of the bark.

A birch tree over sixty inches in diameter cut by beaver. The watch is hung on the stump in order to give a visual proof of the size of the tree.

A typical lodge ready for its final coating of wet sod and mud, which is put on as soon as the nights are cold enough to freeze it.

Others he carried down to the water and swam with them to the harvest pile. Nothing must be wasted. Every shrub or sapling which obstructed the way had to be cut down; if it was not good enough for food it could at least be used in the construction of house or dam. And the beaver continued his work as though he fully realised the importance of doing it well and thoroughly. Occasionally, he was joined by the other members of his family, and the big yellow full moon rising above the tree tops watched the industrious little animals as it had watched their predecessors for thousands of years. With each generation the same work had been carried on with the same persistence, the same regularity and in the same way. The only visible change was that in former years, before man had begun the work of destroying the harmless creatures, and which, since the arrival of the white people of the eastern world, had been so ruthlessly carried on, the beavers did their wood-cutting and dam-building almost as much by daylight as by the light of the stars and moon.* But the little fur-bearers had learned gradually that the sun was not their friend; it offered them no protection from the deadly persecutions of their two-footed enemies, and so they had come to work only under the friendly cover of darkness, or by the

* Although James Hearne, who was a most careful observer, states that, even in the latter half of the eighteenth century, " All their work is done in the night."

soft light of the moon and the twinkling of the stars. Even then, they were always nervously alert, each sound must be understood before it could be ignored. A falling leaf floating almost noiselessly to earth would cause them to desist in their labours, for though they knew full well that during the autumn the leaves, having fulfilled their duties, bid farewell to the slender branches, yet their falling *might* mean the stealthy approach of a man who, touching the tree as he passes, shakes down the dying leaves. The noiseless tread of the deer as it carefully made its way over the velvet carpet of moss they knew, and as it meant no harm, they seldom took notice of it. No man walked liked that. Even the moccasined foot of the Indian made more sound, and set up a vibration on the earth's surface which in no way resembled the delicate footfall of the wild animals. But their enemies, the powerful wolverines, the padded-footed lynx, and the hungry, clever, keen-witted wolf could approach without sound or warning save the scent which they could not disguise. Therefore, when the beaver worked, his mind was divided, and he stopped at frequent intervals to listen, and to test the air for signals of danger, and at the slightest warning he would make his way to the water which offered a safe retreat from nearly all of his enemies. If the danger was imminent, he and all his family could seek safety in the house, and remain there perhaps for the rest of the night, coming out only under water to take some twigs into the house where they could enjoy a meal without fear of pursuit.

But the night passed without mishap, and the first gleam of dawn saw them still busily engaged in their various tasks, hidden from view by the mist which nearly always settles on the ponds during the cool nights.

As the rising sun cleared the air, the beavers, tired after the long night's work, retired to their house, all holding an animated conversation as though discussing the work they had accomplished. Gradually the puppy-like voices died away before the morning breeze disturbed the surface of the pond, and they slept the sleep of those who have worked hard and well, and earned their rest. Let us leave them there to dream of the days when the steel trap will be a thing of the past and they will be able to continue the work which Nature intended they should do.

We have had a glimpse of them in their far-away home and have seen a typical night's employment. Perhaps the question comes to us, Why do they have to work so hard ? Most of the wild animals live a life of comparative ease, thinking only of the day and making no plans, no provision for the morrow. Their food is gathered as it is needed, and most of them have their homes where they happen to be. When tired they seek a sheltered spot and go to sleep, and beyond watching for danger, they trouble themselves but little. But the beaver has definite ideas of what is necessary for his welfare. He plans months ahead. He undertakes stupendous tasks—tasks which demand skill of no mean order. Indeed, some of the most important work done by them may seem at first glance to be superfluous. Why, for instance, does he build dams when water is abundant nearly everywhere within his natural range? Let us, therefore, examine the work and see how it serves a very definite purpose, and having done that we will follow the beaver throughout a few years of their lives and see how they live and how thoroughly their various undertakings work out in the best possible way.

The most conspicuous work, so far as visible results are concerned, is the dam ; and the purpose it serves is not so much to make a swimming pool, as some people imagine, as to keep a body of water at a more or less constant level in order to ensure certain ends : (1) to conceal the entrances to the houses and so prevent the entrance of any land enemies, (2) to be a place for the safe storage of wood for food during the winter, (3) to render the transporting of this wood as simple as possible, and (4) to be a place of retreat in case of attack. To better appreciate the value of the dam it is necessary to understand the structure of the houses, for there are several types. The most primitive is simply a hole in a bank, with no surface work. This repre-

Beaver clearing a roadway.

Beaver lodge cut open to show interior. The lower part is the drying and dining floor; the raised part is the bed. Dimensions (inside), 4 feet 10 inches long, 4 feet 5 inches wide, 2 feet 1 inch high; lower floor, 4 inches above water; bed floor, 6 inches higher.

sents what is probably the original and primitive form of house.   The entrances, for there are usually more than one, are well below the surface of the water.   Then we have the next step in advancement : the hole in the bank with the living chamber coming to the surface, so that in order to make it more secure against marauders and render it drier, a roughly arranged pile of brush, sticks, logs, and mud and grass is heaped over it.   From this it is but a step to the house which is entirely above ground, and placed either on the bank or on an island, and then the final development in which the beavers make the island as a foundation.

In appearance, the two latter types are identical and both have the entrances beneath the water. In building these houses or lodges, as they are more commonly called, the beginning is a composition of mud, brush and small sticks, from which the bark is nearly always eaten.   Whether the mound is placed over the opening of the burrow, or whether the burrow is made after the house has been started, I cannot say with absolute certainty, but from what I have observed of the beginnings of lodges, there seems every reason to believe that the burrow precedes the lodge.   Gradually, as the mound becomes large enough, the inside is hollowed out, then more and more material is added to the outside, larger sticks and even poles or logs are used, all more or less pointing to the apex, so that they support each other to some extent.   Water-soaked grass, roots and mud are employed to fill in the openings, with the result of making the whole structure nearly light-tight and practically water-tight. As soon as the nights are cold enough to freeze, the surface is plastered over with several inches of mud which is usually gathered from the pond or river bottom. This fact, has, I know been questioned even by such authorities as Thompson Seton, who in his excellent book* says: "It (the beaver) never plasters the lodge with mud outside. All lodges are finished outside with sticks." This is more or less true during the earlier part of the season, but in most cases which have come under my observation the houses were thickly plastered over immediately before the actual coming of winter.† The mud, of course, freezes into a solid and intensely hard protective coating—so hard that even the wolves cannot tear a way through; but it breaks away early in the

* "Life Histories of Northern Animals."
† Enos A. Mills, "In Beaver World," states that, "In Montana of twenty-seven beaver houses which I examined twenty-one received mud covering." In Morgan's "The American Beaver" there is the following convincing statement: "Late in the fall, each season, the sides of their lodges, nearly to the summit, are in some cases plastered over with mud, which soon freezing, materially increases their strength." And James Hearne (in (1769—1772) states that: "It is a great part of the policy of these animals to cover, to plaster, as it is usually called, the outside of their houses every fall with fresh mud, and as late as possible in the autumn, even when the frost becomes pretty severe."

spring when softened by the thaw, and the heavy rains wash it off, leaving the outside an untidy mound of sticks and poles. In evidence of this I have made photographs both in Newfoundland and Canada. Some of the houses found in the former country were made almost entirely of mud, sod, and grass, with only a few sticks used in the centre, probably with the idea of leaving the almost inevitable ventilation flue. The form of the lodges varies greatly and it is impossible to lay down any hard and fast rules. Several times I have found houses built surrounding a tree, either living or dead. In such cases the ventilation is afforded by the tree, as the earth and sticks do not adhere very closely to the rough bark. The very idea of making provisions for ventilation is one of the many exhibitions of the clever animals' thoughtfulness. The existence of these ventilation flues has some-times been questioned, but it has been more or less clearly shown in all of the many scores of lodges which I have examined. It is even more notice-able in the winter, when the lodge appears as a mound of snow, a mound like many other irregu-larities in the landscape except that the snow is usually melted or partly melted at the highest point, and on very cold days a thin misty vapour may be seen rising from the place where the flue would naturally be situated. This tell-tale sign is a frequent cause of disaster for the beaver, as it reveals the presence of the lodge to the keen-eyed trapper, who naturally does not hesitate to take the fullest advantage of the information.

Mr. Enos Mills in his delightful book, " In Beaver World," which deals more particularly with the Western States, fully corroborates the fact of the existence of the ventilating flue. He says, " But little earthy matter is used in the tip-top of the house where the minute disjointed airholes between the interlaced poles give the room scanty ventilation." We are of course faced with the question, does the beaver do this intentionally with the realization of what it means? Why not? What reasonable excuse can we have for doubting his understanding of what he is doing. But we must leave this till later when the subject of the intelligence or instinct of the beaver will be treated more thoroughly. At present, the lodge is occupying our attention. Much has been written about these examples of primitive architecture and ridiculous statements have frequently been made. Pictures have appeared (as recently as towards the end of the eighteenth century) which show the houses with two stories, and with windows and doors cut *square*. It will not need much intelligence to see the absurdity of these "facts." First of all, such openings would leave the inmates entirely at the mercy of any passing enemy, and secondly, animals avoid rectangular forms. So the *square* apertures would be practical impossibilities.

A lodge which withstood several weeks' submergence during a flood. In spite of the swift current very little damage was done, though, of course, the beaver had to abandon it for the time.

An unusually large lodge (in Newfoundland) ; it measured 37 feet in its largest external diameter, and was 7 feet high.

Beaver lodge in a swamp concealed among tamarack and firs.

One of the earliest sane descriptions which I have been able to find of a beaver's house appears in the Relations of the Jesuits in Canada. Father Joseph Jouvency, S.J., writes (between the years 1610 and 1613) : " They locate them (the houses) on the banks of lakes and rivers ; they build walls of logs, placing between them wet and sticky sods in the place of mortar, so that the work can, even with great violence, scarcely be torn apart and destroyed. The entire house is divided into several stories.* (*Levels* would probably be a better word); the lowest is composed of thicker crossbeams, with branches strewn upon them, and provided with a hole or small door through which they can pass into the river whenever they wish ; this story extends somewhat above the water of the river, while the others rise higher, into which they retire if the swelling stream submerges the lowest floor. They sleep in one of the upper stories ; a soft bed is furnished by dry sea-weed,† and the moss with which they protect themselves from the cold ; on another floor they have their store-room and food provided for winter. The building is covered with a dome-shaped roof. Thus they pass the winter, for in summer they enjoy the shady coolness upon the shores or escape the summer heat by plunging

* This translation may be questioned ; following is the original version : " *Tota casae fabrica variis contignationibus distinguitur.*"

† *Alga siccior* is the name given, so the translation is open to question.

into the water. Often a great colony of many members is lodged in one house. But, if they be incommoded by the narrowness of the place, the younger ones depart of their own accord and construct houses for themselves." Allowing for slight inaccuracies due to translation, this is a remarkably accurate description and shows what careful observers were those sturdy, self-sacrificing priests who did so much for Canada in her early development. It is all the more extraordinary when we consider how natural history subjects were treated in those days.

The inside of a beaver's lodge is simplicity itself. There is only one chamber, unless possibly two lodges being built adjoining one another may have the rooms connecting. However, this is a condition I have never seen. The size varies, according to conditions, some being as much as twelve feet or more in diameter,* but an ordinary house built to accommodate a family of six would have a room about four or five feet long and rather less in width, with the ceiling at the highest point a little over two feet. The ceiling is fairly smooth, all projecting sticks and roots being carefully cut off. There is, indeed, every evidence to show that the interior is really made and finished after the wall or the mound has been more or less completed. The fact that the sticks are so

---

* Mills gives the size of the chambers as being " from three to twenty feet across."

thoroughly interlaced accounts for the strength of the whole structure, which is arched over with a perfect network, so that when in perfect condition it will bear the combined weight of as many men as could find foothold on it. Even an old lodge may be torn apart so that only a thin shell of the woodwork remains, and yet it will readily bear the weight of a man. In very exceptional cases the domed roof will have a central support built up from the floor, and it is this support which has probably given rise to the stories of many-roomed lodges, for the support is not necessarily a smooth circular column of mud and sticks, but may be an irregular mass which, being added to from time to time, eventually becomes a sort of wall or even a complete partition with one or more openings to allow of communication.

In confirmation of this explanation, there is the following description by Samuel Hearne written between the years 1769 and 1772: "Those who have undertaken to describe the inside of beaver houses, as having several apartments appropriated to various uses, such as eating, sleeping, storehouses for provisions, and one for their natural occasions, etc., must have been very little acquainted with the subject." . . . "Many years constant residence among the Indians, during which I had an opportunity of seeing several hundreds of these houses, has enabled me to affirm that everything of the kind is entirely void of truth." . . . "It

frequently happens, that some of the large houses
are found to have one or more partitions, if they
deserve that appellation; but that is no more than
a part of the main building, left by the sagacity of
the beaver to support the roof.   On such occasions,
it is common for those different apartments, as
some are pleased to call them, to have no communication with each other but by water; so that
in fact they may be called double or treble houses,
rather than different apartments of the same house.
I have seen a large beaver house built in a small
island, that had near a dozen apartments under one
roof; and, two or three of these only excepted,
none of them had any communication with each
other but by water.   As there were beaver enough
to inhabit each apartment it is more than probable
that each family knew its own, and always entered
at their own door."

He goes on to say that his Indians took thirty-
seven beavers out of this house, while many others
escaped.   It is very doubtful whether houses of
this type exist at the present day, nor indeed for
many years past.

The ground floor or lowest level is only three or
four inches above the surface of the water.   This
is used as the "dining-room" and for drying their
coats.   About half of the space is thus occupied,
the other half is raised six or eight inches, and is
the sleeping apartment.   It is well covered with
bedding made of dry grass, which is cut while

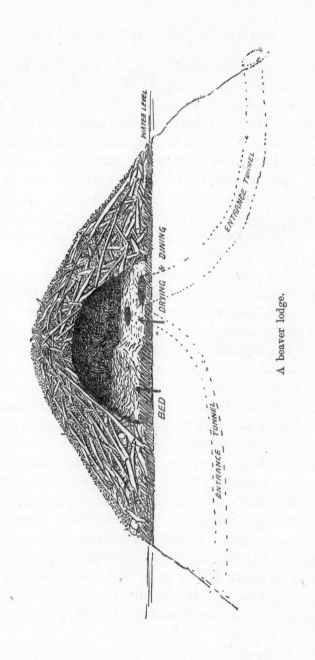

A beaver lodge.

growing, or with shredded wood, the latter being
more frequently employed.   In cutting this bedding, the beaver tears the wood into long strips as
shown in the accompanying illustration.   Whether
or not moss is used, I cannot tell, but in the more
eastern portion of the beavers' range, I have never
seen any in the lodges, nor have I seen the
slightest evidence of its being gathered from the
ground or trees.   However, Mills say that " A
few beds are made of grass, leaves, or moss from
the ground or trees."

Occasionally, houses of immense size are found,
the largest I have actually measured was in
Newfoundland, on the banks of Sandy River.   It
was thirty-seven feet in its greatest diameter and
seven feet in outside height.   For about six years
it had been the home of a colony of beavers,
nine members or perhaps more having occupied it
at one time.   Lodges of this size are extremely
rare, and I can find no record of any that were as
large.   What size the chamber was can only be
conjectured, as I did not feel justified in breaking
into the structure, much as I wished to see the
interior.   In the floor of the lodges are the entrances,
there being usually two, but sometimes three or
even more, their common size varying from ten to
about twenty-five inches in diameter.   The idea
of having more than one is probably to allow of
escape in case of some enemy finding its way in
through one of the burrows.   It also permits of

A typical muskrat's house (Long Island, N.Y.), which closely resembles a very roughly made beaver's lodge, except that reeds instead of logs are used.

Poplar tree cut down by beaver.

An interesting and somewhat unusual type of lodge on the edge of a pond
some distance away from any trees. The lodge is built of mud and
roots taken from the bottom of the pond, and the animals would
probably depend on the roots of water lily and spatter dock for their
winter food (Newfoundland).

Shows an island lodge in a pond made by the beaver.

different members coming in and going out at the same time, as the tunnels are scarcely large enough for the animals to pass each other. Where these tunnels enter the pond, they are more or less arched over with a network of sticks, evidently put there to prevent the burrow falling in. In some instances there is quite a long passage-way cut through a compressed, tangled mass of brush, which was probably originally the remains of a winter food pile. In planning these entrances to the lodge, it is clearly shown that the beaver know what they are about and make provision for their needs with great thoroughness. No sharp bends are made, for that would make it difficult if not impossible, to carry in the sticks which they take into the house to feed on. After all the bark is eaten the bare stick is taken out to be used in the future for building and repairing lodges and dams. Some very small twigs when peeled are worked into the earth for flooring in order to allow for the wear and tear, and keep the floor as dry as possible.

Cleanliness is of course essential where so many animals are confined in such restricted quarters. The beaver are model housekeepers and they allow no dirt or rubbish to accumulate. Everything is neat and tidy, whether the number of inmates is small or large. How they manage to keep it as dry as they do is a marvel when one considers that each time a beaver goes into the lodge he *must* be wet, as his only entrance is through the water. It is obvious therefore that on emerging from the water they must dry themselves off very thoroughly before going near their beds or nests. The fact of their making these beds on a higher level shows that they use their intelligence and understand that water does not run uphill. If the bedding should get wet frequently it would be but a short time before it decayed, especially as there is not a superabundance of air in the houses. Fortunately the beaver has low respiration and consequently needs very little ventilation in his home. On this account he can keep warm, and even during the cold winter weather, when the temperature of the outside air is perhaps thirty or forty degrees below zero, the animal heat generated by the beaver is sufficient to keep the house comfortable. This warmth and the lack of light and air has the disadvantage of causing troublesome parasites to thrive, much to the annoyance of the thickly-furred animals, and probably accounts for their so frequently using shredded wood for bedding. Softer material could be found, but it is doubtful whether it would be sanitary.

The size of the material used on the outside of the lodges is most variable. As already stated, in some instances no sticks of appreciable size are to be found on the lodges. Then, again, regular logs or heavy poles are seen on the lodges. But logs or poles (whichever you like to call them, and it is hard to say where one begins and the other ends) of eighteen feet in length and about six inches in diameter at the larger end are frequently used, and shorter pieces of from one foot in length upwards and having a diameter of eight or nine inches are not uncommon. Just what purpose these short and very heavy pieces serve is difficult to say. They certainly add weight, but is that much advantage? They cannot be said to add to the structural strength, but perhaps when the mud freezes and they become very firmly locked in they offer an insurmountable obstruction to any animal that may attempt the difficult task of digging into the lodge.

As a rule the bulk of the material employed consists of long sticks of one to three inches in diameter at the larger end and a great deal of short stuff of variable size which forms an irregular network. Fibrous roots add greatly to the strength of the work by binding together all the loose material so solidly that it is a task of the utmost difficulty for a man to pull it apart unless he is armed with a pick-axe or crowbar. A well-built lodge will even withstand the destructive power of running water. In Newfoundland I noticed one house while it was being built and remarked on the thoroughness of the work. During the following spring the heavy rains and melting ice and snow caused a flood, which raised the river about eight or ten feet above the normal level. Needless to say the house, whose base was only a foot or so above the ordinary water-line, was entirely submerged, but though the current was swift and continued for several weeks with this unusual depth of water, the structure of the house remained almost intact, only the loose earth and sod being washed away. Of course the beaver had to abandon their home, and they sought temporary shelter in a high bank beneath the roots of some fir trees. Accidents such as these are of frequent occurrence when the lodges are built on the banks of rivers, as the beaver have no control over the depth of water, and such lessons have taught the intelligent animals the advantage of making dams which maintain a more or less constant water level. They learn by sad experience and when they disregard such lessons they have usually to pay heavily for their mistakes.

The river-bank lodges or highly-developed burrows are frequently subject to disaster through rising water, and may be regarded as the work of beavers whose intelligence is somewhat below normal. It is well worth observing that these bank lodges or burrows are most often the homes of solitary beaver, those who, perhaps, through their lower development have been turned out of the colonies to shift for themselves. It is possible, of course, that they are only afflicted with the curse of laziness, but this is doubtful, as it is a somewhat rare fault in wild animals. We have yet much to learn about beaver, and many of our ideas as to the why and wherefore of what they do are based on surmise, which is the result of our very insignificant knowledge.

The situations chosen for the lodges vary entirely with conditions. In some parts of the country the beaver appear to realise the advantage of placing their lodges on the north or north-western side of lakes and streams. By doing this they gain the heat of the sun, which melts the ice away from both bank and lodge and so liberates the animals at the earliest possible date. This I have observed particularly in Newfoundland, where most of the lodges seen during a period of several years were thus situated with apparently no other object in view.

Concealment seems very frequently to be carefully considered, in which cases the lodge is hidden in dense alder thickets or among closely-growing tamarack or spruce. So effectual is the concealment afforded by the scrubby growth that, were it not for the dams or the peeled wood which is found floating near the shore, their existence would be unknown even by those whose eyes are trained to see clearly. As an instance of this, I remember going to see a place where for months some beaver had with untiring persistence built a dam in a railway culvert. Once or twice each week during their activities the section men visited the culvert and pulled out all the accumulation of brush and sod which obstructed the waterway. Where the lodge was they could not tell, though they had gone all through the alder swamps in search of it, and they declared that there was no lodge. This seemed unlikely, as the nature of the land precluded any possibility of a bank burrow. After a careful examination of the vicinity I found it actually on the railway embankment not ten feet from where trains were passing every day, but it was so cunningly hidden in a small, thick clump of alders that it was almost indistinguishable, even though it was fully eight feet in diameter. In complete contrast to this one finds the lodges on the bleakest barrens, away from any trees or shrubs, conspicuous black (being made of pond muck) mounds which are visible for a mile or more. When entirely protected by water there is seldom much attempt at concealment, and one of the most common types is the lodge built on an island, artificial or natural, in the middle of a lake or small pond. So also is the lodge often seen on a bare point of land extending into the lake. As this does not have the protection of the water it makes us wonder whether or not the animals place any importance on concealment, or whether it is simply a matter of individual ideas.

We do not realise sufficiently how strong individuality is in animals when we attempt to generalise or lay down hard and fast rules to govern their actions. It would be far easier for us to under-

A dam in its early stage of construction, showing how the sticks, chiefly alder, are laid lengthways with the stream.

Beaver on the top of his lodge.   It is interesting to note the size of the log in the foreground.   This flash-light exposure was made by the animal.

stand and account for what they do if we would only start out with the idea that both animals and birds, though governed by certain very definite laws, have the use of a limited free intelligence, which enables them to take advantage of conditions and accomplish things which are apparently not in keeping with what might be done by others of the same species. It is this individuality which helps animals to adjust themselves to new conditions, whereas if they adhered too strictly to the rules which have governed them in the past they would, through the lack of power of free thought, fall easy victims to new and adverse conditions.

Having now seen what the beaver's lodge is like, we may take into consideration the dam which is the direct adjunct to the house or rather to the more advanced type of house. Just when or how dams first began it is impossible for us to say, but the chances are they are the result of a very gradual development through perhaps thousands of years. So far as I can learn the beaver of the old world did little or no important dam building, but his close cousin on the American continent has without doubt been building them for a very long time and with some very extraordinary results. (These will be dealt with in another chapter.)

As already stated the primary objects of the dams appear to be four-fold, the most important being apparently that water may be maintained at a constant level in order that the house shall be safe from attack. Whether or not we are correct in our surmise, we know that the dams are built and that they represent by far the most conspicuous work accomplished by any living animal. As feats of engineering skill they must command our highest respect, as examples of industry they are difficult to excel, and as an exhibition of intelligence they are only equalled or perhaps surpassed by the extraordinary, though less conspicuous, canals which are planned and constructed by the same animals.

There have been many fabulous accounts of beaver dams, in the most ridiculous of which the animal has been accredited with " driving stakes as thick as a man's leg into the ground three or four feet deep" and with making regular hurdles on the dams. In fact there has been no limit to the fanciful stories on the subject. Even the generally accurate accounts of Father Joseph Jouvency, S.J. (1610—13), from whom I have already quoted, bear evidence of slight exaggeration. He says, in describing the dams : " If they find any river suitable for their purposes, except in having sufficient depth, they build a dam to keep back the water until it rises to the required height. And first by gnawing them, they fell trees of large size ; then lay them across from one shore to the other. They construct a double barrier and rampart * of logs obliquely placed, having between

* Translation of *Duplicem versum et ordinem arborum faciunt.*

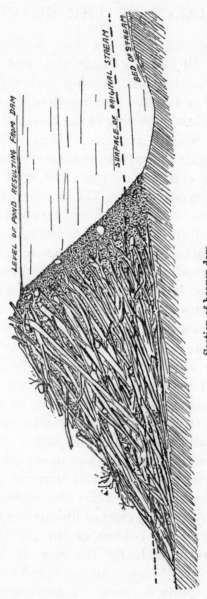

LEVEL OF POND RESULTING FROM DAM

SURFACE OF ORIGINAL STREAM

BED OF STREAM

Section of beaver dam.

R.B.

D

them a space of about six feet, which they so
ingeniously fill in with stones, clay, and branches
that one would expect nothing better from the
most skilful architect.   The length of the structure
is greater or less, according to the size of the stream
which they wish to restrain.   Dams of this kind
a fifth of a mile long are sometimes found."   This
is a strange mixture of truth and error which is
difficult to account for.   The double barrier and
rampart filled in with stones and clay and branches
is very far from the actual construction.   As a
matter of fact, the building of an ordinary dam
consists originally of a number of sticks and brush
being laid (no stakes are driven) in the water with
the butts up-stream.   When slightly weighted
with sod, stones, and water-soaked billets of wood
they become anchored, each projecting twig acting
as a brace against the bottom.   Little by little
more material of the same description is added
until from shore to shore there is an unbroken
line which at first only slightly retards the flow
of the stream.   Then sod and muck, with roots
and grass, are laid against the upper side or face.
By the force of water all this material is worked
in among the network of sticks, the beavers assisting
the water by pushing clots of fibrous muck, usually
gathered from the bottom of the pond, into the
openings until gradually the face of the dams
assumes a smooth appearance levelled to an angle
of about forty-five degrees.   If the work is properly

done, and beavers vary in the quality of their work just as men do, the structure is finally practically watertight. Yet the word *finally* is scarcely the right word to apply to a dam, for so long as the beaver have any need of it they continue adding to both its height and length. What begins by being a perfectly complete dam, perhaps twenty feet long and a foot or two in height, ends with a length of many hundreds of feet and a height of six or seven feet or even more. Besides the above-mentioned materials stones are frequently employed in the construction of dams. In fact it is rare to find any that have not at least a few stones worked in with the sod, particularly towards the ends. When so few are used it is hard to say what purpose they serve. But there are instances of dams being built in which stones form the larger part of the material. These are not common and I have never seen but one example. Unfortunately the photograph shows only those stones which are above water, where there is a fair proportion of other material, but below the surface there was little else than stones of small size, none weighing more than three or four pounds. Very much larger ones are frequently used ; in fact, I have been told by trappers of some that weighed about thirty or forty pounds and even more, and Mills speaks of stones weighing upwards of one hundred and twenty pounds being moved into position on the

dams by the united efforts of many beavers.
Never having seen any heavier than nine pounds,
I cannot guarantee the correctness of the trappers'
statement, but Mills is a careful and very accurate
observer and thoroughly reliable.   Generally speaking, it is not wise to be too incredulous, and any
information, to have value, should be the result of
very careful, personal observation.   Otherwise the
source of the information should be given.   Many
of the trappers are blessed with a keen and rather
subtle sense of humour, and few things give them
greater pleasure than filling up the stranger with
yarns, and they derive a real joy if they ever
happen to see these same yarns in print, especially
if the "facts" are given as though they were
entirely original with the writer.   On more than
one occasion has a trapper told me of how he had
tricked the tenderfoot into believing most fabulous
stories of the ways of wild animals.   Some of
course tell of strange happenings, not with the idea
of having fun, but they enlarge on already much
enlarged stories that have been retailed to them.
Few stories shrink in the telling, while most grow
with alarming vigour, and if we would believe all
that is told of beavers our minds would be filled
with most marvellous "facts" more wonderful,
even though less reasonable, than what is accomplished by these interesting animals.

In practically everything that is done by them
we can, if we use a little care, discover the object,

A very much curved dam.

Dam built almost entirely of small stones, weight of which seldom exceeded 4 lbs.

Where the beaver have cut grass for bedding (Newfoundland).

and though at first glance we might sometimes be led to imagine that improvement could be made in the method, if we go far enough into the question and thoroughly appreciate the animal's point of view, his needs and the natural restrictions of his ability, we are nearly always forced to acknowledge the success of his methods. Certainly in the building of the dams, improvement both in the choice of site and the actual execution of the work is most difficult to suggest. Indeed it is very doubtful whether the average man could, without tools, or even with the help of an axe, overcome the obstacles which are encountered by the beaver.

Most writers in dealing with the subject are inclined to pay too much importance to the curve of a dam. Some assume that all dams are built with the curve against the current, others that such is the case only when the flow of water is swift, while some claim that the curve is most often down stream. I have seen a great many dams built in many different situations and under very different conditions, and the conclusion which has been forced on me is that there is no rule to govern the curve. It just happens. I have seen quite large dams, two or three hundred feet long, which were almost straight, others had a decided curve up stream. Others again, under apparently similar conditions, were curved with the current, while on more than one occasion the dam has been like a drawn-out letter S, that is to say with half of it curving up and the other half down stream. On the whole, I think the subsidiary or supporting dams are more likely to be straight or have the curve away from the main structure. These subsidiaries are of very great interest, as they offer a clear example of the beaver's forethought, that is, if we are right in our conclusions, for we believe that they are placed below the most important dam in order to support it, by backing the water against its base, and also for the protection it gives when the pond is frozen, for then the mass of ice which forms in the usually quiet water acts as a powerful support to the principal structure, which has to resist a terrific pressure of ice, snow and water, especially at the time when winter is breaking up. But there are probably other reasons for the existence of these extra structures. It will be noticed that frequently there are a number of them—sometimes as many as eight or more at distances apart which may vary from a few feet up to several hundred. Some are of quite imposing size, while others may be only insignificant affairs a foot or two long and very roughly built. Between each dam, there is usually water of sufficient depth to allow the beaver to hide and so escape his enemies. Then again there is another important reason for these lesser dams. No matter how well the main structure is built, how carefully it is designed, an unusually heavy volume of water may cause it to break. The result of such a calamity would be that the pond would be lowered and the entrances to the lodges exposed, perhaps even the beaver would be left without any place of retreat. The subsidiary dams would greatly lessen the dangers as they would retain the water to a greater or lesser depth according to the conditions. There would be still another advantage in holding back the water, as it would make the repair work or rebuilding of the main dam a matter of much less difficulty owing to the decreased force of the current. Taking all things into consideration, we can see how important are these secondary or supporting dams and how greatly they reflect credit on the animal's power of reasoning and application of this power. For by doing what apparently is a vast amount of extra and, at first glance, almost unnecessary work, the beaver is taking steps to prevent a possible catastrophe. Surely he must reason this out, for otherwise how would he know that great rains do come, and even the greatest dams do burst. Does he learn it by seeing some of the very small structures give way under pressure slightly more than normal? But who shall answer these questions?

In building the smaller dams, the method of construction differs in no way from that already described; only in point of size are they different. As a rule they are not large, seldom more than about thirty feet in length. Exceptions there are to this, but speaking generally, they are below this

length, while the height is in accordance with the
demands of the stream. The more rapid the
current the higher the dam. In very flat country,
where the waterways are sluggish, and these are
the most sought after by the beaver, they are
usually not more than a foot or two in height.
Few streams are too large, and none too small for
dams. I have seen a stream less than two feet
wide on which there were no less than seven
within a distance of scarcely one hundred yards.
Their chief object, apparently, was to keep the
water from draining out of a flat alder swamp,
from which the beavers were busily engaged in
getting their winter supply of food. To have
hauled branches through the tangled undergrowth
would have been a difficult task, but by keeping
the water only a few inches above its normal level
they could make channels among the hummocks
through which they could with comparative ease
swim with the branches and sticks.

In selecting the site for the dam, the beaver
shows a remarkable power of discrimination, and
one wonders how it is that so short an animal can
possibly make any survey of the country and get
any appreciation of the conditions. They have
two principal objects in view when selecting the
site for a new house; an abundance of water, and
trees whose bark is suitable for food. These are
their needs, but the question of obtaining and
controlling them requires serious consideration and

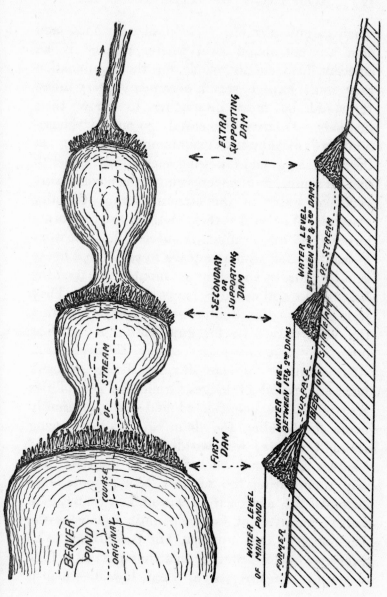

Arrangement of main and subsidiary dams in plan and section.

much careful planning. Good sites for house and dam are not found everywhere, neither is an adjacent food supply, while for the combination they must have to search over many weary miles. It would be most interesting to know their methods. Do they deliberately go out on " house-hunting " expeditions, examining everything as they go along, and following each stream either to find its source, or discover springs which will ensure sufficient water in the stream during the dry season ? Whatever is their method, the results are in nearly all cases eminently successful. The work of hunting for a suitable place to establish a house is done during the summer months, for then the beavers do not usually occupy their lodge. They wander about the country, nearly always following the waterways. If, for any reason, it is their intention to found a new colony, they remain in what seems a desirable situation, living in bank burrows instead of lodges, while the possibilities are thoroughly investigated and plans apparently made for building the dam. A stream flowing through country well wooded with poplars and hardwoods is usually chosen, and the work begins at any time during the summer, though more often towards the approach of autumn. Sometimes, indeed, no attempt is made until as late as the beginning of cool weather, but there seems to be every reason for believing that they prefer the time when the streams are at their lowest, which is

A subsidiary or supporting dam.

Mending a broken dam.

August. Then they see what is the minimum supply of water, and the dam may be built with the least possible trouble. When they finally settle on the exact site, the first sticks are laid, and these in most cases are freshly cut and not peeled. Alders are perhaps the most frequently used, as they are found growing along the waterways and are therefore easily obtained, while their weight allows of their being sunk without much difficulty, and their irregular form of growth helps them to hold on the bottom against the current of water. How quickly a dam is built depends entirely on the urgency of the situation. If it is late in the year, the building proceeds with incredible speed, little more than a week of steady work on the part of a family will see a thirty or forty-foot dam raised to a height of two feet or more. As soon as it backs up the water, the house is commenced and we find that all the different tasks are being attended to simultaneously—dams, both main and subsidiary, lodges, tree-cutting, and storing of winter food. Within a few weeks the colony becomes established and the face of the land is changed by the work of these small animals. Larger and larger the pond grows, as the dam is extended, while the banks are covered with fresh, white stumps of fallen trees, as though a gang of lumber-men were at work. Each night sees marked changes resulting from the untiring work of these builders and tree-cutters. If the colony is successful and the site chosen proves entirely satisfactory it will continue to grow as the years go on, each year seeing the extending of the dam, and, if necessary, the number of subsidiary dams increased. The trees whose base has been flooded by the rising water gradually die, and the gaunt grey columns bear witness to the effect that beavers' work has on the land. So long as the supply of suitable food trees is to be found the colony remains, unless killed off or driven off by the trappers, and so it is that such immense dams are found, some over two thousand feet in length with a height of from two to about fourteen feet, the result of countless generations of industrious beavers, not necessarily working continuously, for they often abandon a pond for many years, apparently to give time for the food trees to grow. On their return, or if a new colony takes possession, they have a busy time repairing the dam and getting everything in proper order.

The solidity of the structures is perhaps best proved by the fact that some have been found in Montana which were in a partially petrified state. As a rule, however, the life of a dam is but a few years beyond the period during which it is used ; owing to the nature of the material employed, constant supervision and repair are absolutely necessary. The beaver realise this and seldom allow a night to pass, during the autumn, without making a tour of inspection and building up and strengthening any part that shows signs of weakness. The smallest hole is soon enlarged by the pressure of water passing through, so that if it is not speedily closed the destruction of the whole structure is threatened ; rats, musquash and otters sometimes burrow through the dams and cause untold damage.

How persistent the beaver is in repairing is well illustrated by the following experiment made in the Algonquin Reserve. Knowing that the best way to secure flashlight photographs of the animals at work was by making a break in their dam, I selected one within convenient distance of where I was staying. After arranging the cameras in position, I made an opening in the dam about two feet wide and laid a thread across. This was attached to the electric switch which operated the flashlight and shutters of the cameras. Scarcely three hours elapsed before the animals, who had found that the water was rapidly escaping from their pond, visited the dam and repaired the breach. Before midnight I returned and reset the cameras, after again opening the dam. Before morning this had again been mended. After that I continued each night to repeat the operation, breaking open the dam at least once each night, sometimes twice, and on two occasions three times. During the twenty-two nights, only twice did the beaver fail to more or less completely fill in the openings I had made, though they never once did so while I remained to watch, even though I took every possible precaution not only to conceal myself, but to select a position down wind of the dam, where I remained sometimes during the greater part of the night.

When a dam is abandoned, it is soon worn down by animals using it as a roadway, or it is overgrown by alders and willows, whose roots cause a certain amount of leakage, so that the pond is gradually drained, and in a very few years there is little to show that a dam ever existed in the place.

Among the many interesting features of the dams, there is one which speaks most highly for the builder's intelligence. That is the method adopted for taking care of the overflow. In most cases, the water finds its way through the loose brush near the crown. This is well enough under normal conditions, but when the dam is on a good-sized stream so that there is a large volume flowing from the pond, the beaver frequently make a spill-way or opening a few feet wide, and deep according to the conditions. These openings are quite clearly defined, and are evidently made with a full under-standing of their purpose. For when there is a scarcity of water, the intelligent animals close the opening as much as may be necessary. This shows how thoroughly they realise what they are doing when building their dams, and how they understand the value of controlling the outlet of the water. They are always ready to grapple with new problems, and no ordinary contingency appears to baffle them.   I saw an instance in Newfoundland which may be worth repeating : a small colony of beaver were engaged in building a dam across a swift stream about forty feet in width. Before the work was quite finished, so that the dam had not yet settled enough to gain its proper strength, there came a great rain which continued for several days and flooded the country. The beavers, seeing that their new dam was threatened with immediate destruction, came down during the night and made a large opening by cutting away the sticks. This allowed the water to escape and so the dam was saved. No sooner had the water resumed its normal level than the little engineers closed the break they had made and continued the structure to its completion. For fear that I might have been mistaken and that the opening had been made by the force of the water, I examined it carefully and found the tooth-marks on the sticks showing without doubt where the animals had cut them away : and it is of interest to note that Father Jouvency, as long ago as 1610—13, made note of this same thing being done. He says : " But if the river swell more than is safe, they break open some part of the structure, and let through as much water as seems sufficient."

The more we study the beaver dams the more we must recognise the care exercised in the selection of their sites. Everything seems to be considered and every advantage is taken of the prevailing conditions. In the photograph there is an example of how cleverly the small creatures utilised an immense boulder in the middle of a rapid flowing stream. Rocky bedded waterways offer many and serious difficulties to the beavers, for it is hard to get anchorage, and in this particular case the current was so swift that to build a successful dam required unusual skill. Evidently the beaver made a thorough investigation of the little river and finally selected what was about the only reasonably good place for their operations. The large boulder acted as a support or anchor for their work (this can be plainly seen in the photograph), so that when the structure, which was over four feet high, was finished, it resisted the flow of water and formed a fair-sized pond and an island on which the beaver built their lodge.

Some writers have claimed that the animals begin their dams by felling a large tree across the stream. This may be true, but I have never seen an instance of it. What does often happen is that a fallen tree lying across a stream suggests a good position for the dam, or a floating log carried down during the spring thaws becomes lodged against the stream banks so that the beaver take advantage of it and build against it. Except under conditions of this kind it is unusual to find the timber, whether stick, brush or log, placed so that it lies in any way but with the course of the stream. This is reasonable enough when we consider how little

Beaver in the act of repairing a break in the dam.   The animal himself fired the flash by touching a thread.

A gate or spillway cut in the dam in order to let the surplus water escape. In times of drought this would be either partly or completely closed.

Showing the facing of a recently abandoned dam.

cross-pieces would add to the strength of the dam,
and they would be easily dislodged by the pressure
of the flowing water. Whereas when placed with
butts upwards and headed against the current, the
points are forced against the bed of the river and
as weight is added to them they offer a barrier of
great strength, capable of resisting any ordinary
pressure of water. When the supply of water is
too limited, the beaver take the utmost care to see
that none is wasted, and the dam is coated with
unusual care to render it practically watertight
even towards the ends, and every tiny trickle is
stopped, sometimes by little dams only a few
inches long, just a handful or two of sod placed in
exactly the right position, perhaps some distance
from the actual structure. If during the autumn
these are trodden down or broken they will nearly
always be repaired within a few hours, so careful
is the supervision of the beaver.

For some reason which can only be guessed at,
the beaver nearly always leave a roadway across
the dam leading from the pond to the outlet. This
is also much used by other animals of aquatic
habits such as mink, musquash and otter, and
though occasionally we also find a well-beaten
path running along the dam from bank to bank
this is not a beaver path. More often it is the
work of foxes, deer, lynx and other prowlers of
the woods, as well as man, who finds these
" bridges " most convenient. Many a time have

I found myself at a loss for a way of crossing a stream until the fortunate discovery of a beaver dam has enabled me to avoid a wetting.

Having now seen something of the dams, so that without going into a lot of tiresome and unnecessary detail such as exact measurements of numerous structures (which must vary continually), the reader has at least a general idea of what they are like without, I hope, being too much bored. We have seen that the dams range in length from a few inches to two thousand feet or more, and in height up to fourteen feet, containing from a pound or two of building material up to several hundred tons, all carried laboriously by the industrious builders in their tiny hands or with their powerful teeth. Also that the idea of this stupendous work is to enable the animals to keep water at a constant level for the protection of their lodge and to furnish them with a convenient means of transporting their supply of wood. This brings us naturally to their wood-cutting operations, about which many wonderful tales have been told. Before going into the methods, it might be well to give the reason for woodcutting even at the risk of slight repetition. Beavers' natural food consists of a purely vegetable diet, the chief item being the bark of trees, not the outside shell, but the cambium layer which contains the very life of the tree. To a limited extent they also use the wood itself, but the nutriment obtained from it is so insignificant that it is only occasionally used. Nearly all of the deciduous or broad-leaved trees supply food for the beaver, but the most sought-after are perhaps the different birches, maples, poplars, willows and ashes—to a less extent, alder, viburnum, dog-wood, wild cherry and others according to the locality. The bark of the conifers is not much used, some authorities say that it is never eaten, yet the trees are frequently cut down by the beaver. I have seen several instances, but none of them had any of the branches cut off. From Indians and trappers, I have been told that immediately before the young are born or about that time, the prospective mother eats a small amount of spruce, pine or other conifer bark, which they believe to have some medicinal property. During the spring and summer, many kinds of roots and berries are eaten, and at all seasons the roots of water-lily and spatterdock are used. In certain districts these form the main supply even during the winter, when the beaver come out of the lodges, and beneath the ice gather the roots as they are needed and take them into their houses to eat. From this habit has come the curious superstition that a beaver if shot in the evening sinks, while if shot in the morning he floats, because he is filled with the light, pithy substance of the lily root which has been eaten during the night. Needless to say, this is scarcely likely to be true, though, as I have never shot a beaver, I cannot speak from actual experience. Now it will be noted

that bark is the chief food, and that in order
to obtain a supply sufficient to carry the animals
over the long, dreary, snow-bound winter months
a quantity must be stored. Needless to say,
this necessitates the felling of trees and saplings before the cold weather comes. A certain
amount of brush is used from which the tender
bark is eaten, and most of this brush is obtained
from the ends of branches, although some shrubs
are also cut. Apparently not so much bark is eaten
during the spring and summer as later, if we may
judge from the peeled sticks which are found in
such abundance in September, October and November. During the earlier part of this season, no wood
is stored, though many trees are either cut or partly
cut, while still more are simply marked or blazed,
as already stated in the beginning of this volume.
This blazing at first glance reminds one of the work
of the lumber-man and we are inclined to put a
wrong construction on beavers' ideas. We might
think that the trees are simply being marked for
cutting later on, or that the head of the family or
colony selects what trees he considers should be
felled and marks them with the three or four cuts.
But though such theories are most alluring, and
one is surprised that they have not led to additional
stories of beaver-wonders, common sense steps in
and offers a logical reason which should be considered, even though it is merely practical and not
at all particularly wonderful. This explanation is

Recently made dam.

A prolonged rain flooded the stream and threatened to carry away the dam, so the beaver made an opening through which the water escaped and the dam was saved. The opening was afterwards closed.

Two subsidiary or secondary dams.

The same dam as shown in previous illustration, but seen from above in order that the opening made by the beaver might be more clearly seen.

that in order to keep the bark perfectly sweet while under water for a considerable time, the tree must be in a certain condition, otherwise the bark might ferment or in some other way become unfit for food. The only way in which the beaver can assure himself of the tree's condition is by biting into the inner bark, therefore this would account for the numerous blazed trees which may be found in the vicinity of the ponds and lodges. Carrying this idea a little further, we have also a possible explanation for the fact that such a large number of trees are girdled and left often for weeks before being finally dropped. This girdling allows the tree to dry more quickly than if left with the bark on. The acceptance of this theory means, of course, that we are endowing the animals with extraordinary intelligence; but how can we avoid doing so when we see what they accomplish? When I first described this systematic marking of trees, I was ridiculed, partly because it had not previously been brought to anyone's notice (so far as I know), but the fact that it is commonly done by beavers can be proved by a visit to any place where the animals are preparing to store their winter food, and as a reason for its being done these theories are offered simply as theories.

It has often been said that cutting down trees is the most wonderful work accomplished by beaver, but how such a conclusion can be reached is difficult to understand. Nearly all of their efforts demand far greater intelligence, though from a physical point of view the cutting of immense trees by so small an animal is extraordinary, if not unique in the world of quadrupeds. Just as in all their other engineering and architectural feats, the beaver are most systematic in their wood-cutting operations; as a rule the trees bordering the pond or river are the first to be cut, then as this supply is depleted they go further afield; but as the carrying and pushing of logs on land is hard work they clear a path or road to the water. When they discover a place where there is a poplar grove or clump of suitable trees of any variety, they will, before beginning other work, make a smooth road-way, often as much as five feet or more in width leading from the trees to the nearest water. From this road every obstruction will usually be cleared so that the logs may be brought down with the least possible effort. The actual cutting down of the tree is done by means of the chisel-like teeth which cut through the wood across the grain with the keenness of steel. The number of beaver that work together is variable, often a solitary one unaided will cut down a tree eight or ten inches in diameter during a single night, sometimes several will work together; though it is most unusual for more than two to be actually cutting at the same time, others may be near by, and even take turns, but they avoid getting in each other's way. It has often been said that while a tree is being cut, one beaver stays some distance away and watches the top. At the first intimation of its falling, he signals by either slapping the ground or the water with his tail and the others immediately run away. Unfortunately, I have never been an eye-witness of such a performance, and even though I have heard many trees being felled—some within forty yards of my camp—I have never heard the signal, nor have I seen the beaver on watch. Besides which, it scarcely seems reasonable that the animal while cutting should need any notice of the tree falling. With his teeth against the wood, the creaking sound of even the beginning of the fall would be very evident, even if he did not hear the top brushing against the other trees on its downward path. Animals do not do unnecessary things, and this warning certainly seems unnecessary even though it may be true. That the beavers remain fairly quiet for a few minutes after a tree has crashed to earth is quite possible, though it is not by any means always done, while the explanation usually offered does not sound altogether right. Why should the sound of a falling tree attract enemies? Such sounds are only too common in the forests, and the noise made by the biting of the wood is so loud that even a man with his dulled sense of hearing can distinguish it many hundred yards away on a still night. If the beaver does stay motionless after the crash there is probably some other reason—possibly it is for

the purpose of resting. From the very different
heights of the stumps it is obvious that the
beaver follows no hard and fast rule in cutting.
Frequently stumps four or five feet in height are
found. These of course are done when the ground
is covered with well-packed or ice-coated snow,
except in cases where the animal stands on a convenient log or mound of earth, and so reaches high
enough to avoid the bulging part of the trunk near
the ground. That the beaver ever make piles of
earth for the purpose of having an elevated plat-
form is hard to believe, notwithstanding what has
been written on that subject. The origin of such
stories is probably the mounds of moss-covered
earth or decayed tree stumps which are so often
found close against growing trees, marking perhaps
the tombstone of the parent of the existing tree.
These mounds are quickly worn down by the
beaver standing on them so that they have the
appearance of being made of freshly collected mud
or earth.

In cutting, the beaver sometimes stands erect
and cuts as high as he can reach, then again, judging from the very low stumps, some of them
stand on all fours, but the usual method is to
stand on the hind feet with the broad tail stretched
out behind to act as a balance. Either one or
both front feet or hands are placed on the trunk.
In most cases, the cutting is done all round the
tree as shown in some of the photographs, while

occasionally, owing to the position of the tree, the cutting is done entirely from one side. This, of course, involves far greater labour on account of the larger opening being necessary. The size of the chips which are cut by the beaver is truly extraordinary. If the wood is soft, such as poplar or cedar, they will take out pieces fully five inches long by an inch and a half wide and three quarters of an inch in thickness, while with hard woods such as maple or birch, the chips will be usually three to four inches long and one and a half wide. Much larger chips are sometimes found, but they are exceptional, and must not be taken as the rule. Nine inch chips are mentioned by some writers, but they were perhaps cut for bedding purposes, to be taken in the lodge and shredded, and can not, therefore, be regarded as chips cut during the felling of trees. From the size of the tooth scars, the size of the beaver may be judged. Many other tales do they tell. Often the mark of a chipped tooth is found, which shows that the animal had probably been caught in a trap and broken the tooth by trying to bite the cruel steel, while dull and rough edges are evidence of the great age of the beaver, just as the narrow cuttings are the work of the youngsters.

The upsetting of pet beliefs is always a thankless task; but this is not a book of fairy tales. The truth, so far as possible, must be told even at the risk of being called to account for being too practical and not indulging sufficiently in romance. The popular notion that the beaver knows exactly in which direction a tree will fall is not borne out by fact, and I feel sure, after having made a careful study of the subject, that the direction is purely a matter of chance. It is quite true that most trees growing near the water fall towards it, but this is not due in any way to the wishes or skill of the animal, but to the obvious fact that trees grow towards light. The water, being an open space, attracts them ; therefore when cut it is only natural that they should fall the way they are inclined. Another common fallacy is that the beaver never makes mistakes in tree cutting. Quite a large proportion of the trees they cut lodge in the branches of their neighbours. When this happens they are usually abandoned without further effort, but sometimes we see cases which prove the persistence of the little woodsmen. Not only will they cut through the trunk a second time, but even a third or fourth time, in the hopes of attaining their object. The photograph shows a good example of this. The tree, a birch, ten inches in diameter at the stump, was cut through twice without bringing it down. A third attempt was made, but not quite completed at the time that the photograph was taken. It is not to be wondered at that the little creatures should make such mistakes, considering the fact that their eyesight is only fairly good, and that as they work almost entirely

In this rapid stream (Newfoundland) the beaver selected the only possible place for their dam. By making use of the large boulder they secured anchorage for the structure.

The log (cut by lumber-men) seen in the foreground evidently suggested to the beaver the site for their dam, and is an illustration of how they take advantage of conditions. The dam was 365 feet in length.

A birch tree that lodged. The stump is shown on the right side. When cut the tree became caught by upper branches and only dropped to where it is seen near the stump. Another cutting was made, but the tree still remained entangled and the trunk fell but a few feet, as seen on the left side. The third attempt, which was not completed, is shown in the inclined trunk.

during the night they can scarcely be expected to see clearly the tree-tops which are perhaps forty or fifty feet above them. How often does man make exactly the same mistake ? Yet he works in broad daylight and has far better eyesight. When a tree becomes lodged, the beavers' method of solving the difficulty is usually quite different from our own. We seldom cut through the same tree a second time, but choose rather to cut away the obstructing tree. The beaver, on the contrary, nearly always confines his efforts to bringing down the tree he wants by repeated cutting. Only very rarely do they adopt the man's method. In cases where a tree falls so that it comes nearly to the ground either through being entangled in another tree or held up by its own branches resting on the ground, the beaver make their way along the inclined trunk and cut off the supporting branches or, if not too thick, the top of the tree, so that it shall fall to earth and be more easily manipulated. The great weight of the beavers' body and the formation of their feet prevent their climbing a vertical trunk, but when it inclines to an angle of even forty degrees they manage to walk along the rough bark without difficulty. Often have I found branches cut off which were eight or ten feet from the ground, but seldom at any greater height.

The size of trees which beaver will cut is almost incredible. The largest I have seen was twenty-two inches in diameter where the cut was made,

that is to say, about sixty-six inches in circumference, a tree large enough to give an amateur axe-
man a lot of trouble. There are accounts of still
larger trees being brought down by the industrious
little woodsmen. Lewis and Clarke mention having
found trunks which measured nearly three feet in
diameter, and Mills says : " The largest beaver-cut
stump that I have ever measured was on the
Jefferson River, in Montana, near the mouth of
Pipestone Creek. This was three feet six inches in
diameter." He omits to mention the species of
tree, but it was probably a cotton-wood, as it is
impossible to imagine the animals attempting to
cut anything harder when the immense size is
considered. A tree having a circumference of
approximately 126 inches must offer almost insurmountable difficulties, but, when successfully felled,
the animals would at least experience the satisfaction
of having a very liberal supply of food, enough
perhaps to last a family all winter. Trees of these
sizes are of course exceptional ; the usual size ranges
from four to ten or twelve inches in diameter. These
are more convenient to handle, and in the end offer
a more economical undertaking, as they can be cut
up and every part, including trunk and branches,
can be used, whereas if the trunk is too large, they
never attempt to cut it into short lengths suitable
for transporting to the food pile. Seldom indeed
do they divide a trunk having a maximum diameter
of more than eight or nine inches. Even this size

necessitates a great deal of labour, as, in order that they may be easily handled, the logs must be very short, not longer in fact than a foot and a half or two feet. The beaver knows the weight of wood to a nicety, and he divides the logs and branches into lengths which can be handled. This, one may say, is instinctive. Perhaps so. But it looks uncommonly like reasoning. It certainly requires something very closely akin to intelligence to work out the weight of a long prostrate log, so that as the diameter decreases the distance between cuts increases, with the result that each piece is of more or less the same weight. There is nothing haphazard about it, and though the beaver have no callipers or measures, they seem to know by looking at the log what proportion the length should have to the diameter, and seldom do may make any very great mistake in their calculations. Abandoned logs are found, but whether left on account of their excessive weight or from some other cause we cannot say for certain. It is more than likely that the wretched creatures become so absorbed in their labours that they fail to detect the stealthy approach of some enemy, and so fall easy victims, the forsaken log remaining to mark the place of the pitiful tragedy. The methods adopted by the beaver for taking the logs down to the water are various. When the branch is small, or long and thin, it is usually carried in the teeth, the larger end forward if it has many twigs, otherwise the smaller and

lighter end is held in the teeth so that the remainder
hangs over the animal's shoulder. Sometimes the
beaver proceeds in this way on his hind feet only,
with his front feet or hands holding the branch.
Heavier logs are pulled or pushed either with the
head, chest or even the hips. Whether more than
one does this work I have never been able to assure
myself, but I think it is usual for a single beaver to
take complete charge of his own log, get it down
to the water as best he can, and then swim with it
to the wood pile, where he sinks it or places it on
the top, according to his own ideas. How the
sinking of the wood is done has given rise to many
fanciful tales. Some trappers firmly believe that
they suck the air out of the wood so that it will
easily sink. Anything more absurd would be hard
to imagine. As a matter of fact, all the hard
woods have a specific gravity nearly equal to that
of water, so it requires very little effort to take
them down. Many a time have I watched the
beaver swimming across their pond with a branch,
and on arriving at the food pile dive under water,
taking their branch with them. How they manage
to keep the wood from floating is somewhat difficult
to understand, but they succeed in doing so most
effectively. I have never seen the short, thick logs
carried down. They appear to be forced under
water by the weight of other material which is piled
on top of them. The size of the wood piles varies
according to the number of beaver who are expected

An abandoned beaver dam over 300 feet long.

A tree which was evidently cut when the ground was covered with snow, as the top of the stump is over four feet high.

Stump on a dam cut from the surface of snow.

to subsist on them, and to the severity of the winter in each neighbourhood. Some piles are fully thirty-five or even forty feet across and contain a fairly closely-packed mass of browse and wood from five to about ten feet in depth. Very little use is made of this store, or what remains of it, after the ice melts, for then the beaver prefers to cut fresh material for food. The water-soaked mass of brush is generally left at the bottom where, by rotting, it gradually settles lower and lower, and often forms a foundation for a new house or anchorage for the next season's cuttings. Occasionally trees are dropped into the water, more particularly in rivers, so that the tops as well as a large part of the branches are submerged. The beaver leave them there, knowing full well that they can come whenever they wish during the winter and cut off what they need under water. It is usually noticeable that when a tree is used in this way the animals cut off much of the bark around the thicker portion of the trunk, whether it is exposed or beneath the water, and they also trim the tree of most of the branches which project above water.

When the lodges are built in places where there is a swift current, few trees of any size are ever cut below the lodges. Well do the animals know that swimming with heavy branches against the stream is hard work and usually quite unnecessary, so they do practically all their wood-cutting above stream and often let the heavier logs drift down until they are nearly opposite the lodge or store, when they are immediately steered to where they are wanted. Still further do they go in their practical understanding of water transport, and perhaps I can explain this best by means of the accompanying sketch. It will be observed that the lodge is at a bend in the river on the upper end of a back eddy, so that where the winter wood-pile is placed there is practically no current. The beaver were getting their supply of wood very largely from a small grove of birches on the further side of the pond which had its outlet in the river at a point where the current was flowing rapidly down stream, so that to have taken the wood to the winter pile by way of this opening would have necessitated a long swim against the current. Instead of this, however, the beaver made a roadway across the narrowest part of the neck of land to a place *where the return eddy ran toward the lodge*. No man could have worked out the problem with greater reason. It might be suggested that this is an exceptional example. But such is not the case, for practically similar exhibitions of the beavers' engineering skill are to be seen wherever the little creatures are found. In places where there is a high bank separating the pond from the river, they will cut a tunnel through large enough to enable them to swim to the river and carry their branches without difficulty. A short cut would not be of much avail if it meant

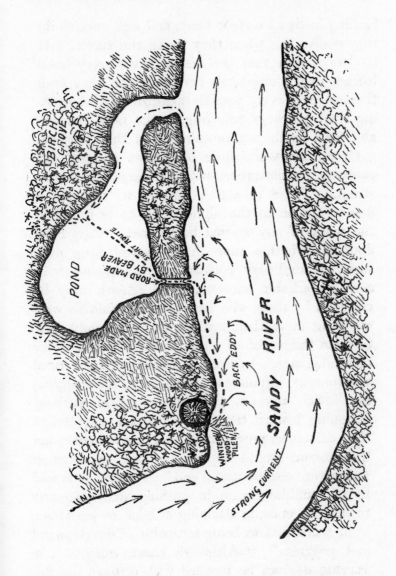

hauling loads up a steep bank, and well enough do they realise this when they make the tunnel. It is always seen that the beaver never carry wood further than is absolutely necessary, and they avail themselves of every possible opportunity of shortening their journeys, resorting to the most remarkable feats for the accomplishment of their purpose.

Of all the work done by beaver nothing can compare for cleverness with the canals they construct. These canals, I venture to say, are a demonstration of the highest skill to be found in the work of any animal below man. It is even doubtful whether man in his lowest form does such extraordinary constructive work, and with such remarkable success. This remark may be criticised by those who hate to credit animals with anything more than instinct, and absolutely deny to them the power of a certain very definite order of intelligence. Instinct is defined as " a natural spontaneous impulse or propensity, especially in the lower animals, that moves them without reasoning toward the actions that are essential to their existence, preservation and development, and that reason would approve as tending to their welfare or to some useful end." Further, it is said to be " unlike reason in pushing unintelligently toward its ends, in attaining at once to perfection in its work, and as being incapable of development and progress." "Although reason may . . . in varying degrees be blended with *instinct*, the distinction between the two is sufficiently precise; for reason, in whatever degree present, only acts upon a definite and often laboriously acquired knowledge of the relation between means and ends." If we accept these definitions how can we possibly avoid crediting the beaver with the power of reasoning? In so much that they do they surely prove a clear understanding "of the relation between means and ends." Do they go to all the trouble of building dams, and making great canals without a full realisation of what is to be gained by the labour? They are not actually doing anything which can be said to directly affect their welfare, but something which *when completed* will reduce their labours and enable them to carry on certain undertakings with *the least possible effort and the best possible results.* It seems to prove that they think ahead and make their plans accordingly. When man builds a bridge across a river he does so simply to enable him to have access to the two sides with the least effort. It is not necessary to his existence any more than are the canals which intersect the country, so that produce may be carried from place to place with the greatest ease. He is doing exactly what the beaver does, and yet no one would venture to say that we build bridges and canals by instinct. We say that we have thought the matter out very carefully, and have acted according to reason, while the poor beaver, which does what are practically the same things on even a greater scale when one considers their size and the restrictions due to lack of implements, acts only by instinct. It is indeed difficult to understand the discrepancy. We might say with some reason that the cutting down of trees is the result of instinct, just as an elephant reaches a branch with his trunk and pulls it down so that he may enjoy eating the leaves which would otherwise be out of reach, or a rat eats his way through an oat bin in order to get at the contents. The results in such cases are obvious, they require no great thought or abstract reasoning, they are the result of an immediate desire for, or need of, food, the search for which is a primal instinct born in all forms of animal life, and manifesting itself long before there can be the slightest development of reason. The young of many birds are blind when first hatched, yet they know enough by inherited instinct to hold up their heads and open their mouths when food is brought. So also the sightless young of many animals have practically but one way of expressing consciousness, which is to suckle. So the actual obtaining of food in an obvious way is easily accounted for by instinct; but when animals plan against emergencies which are *bound* to come some months ahead, or against contingencies which may *possibly* come, they are reasoning to a greater or lesser degree according to the methods employed for making the necessary provisions.

In certain ways, the beaver is a low order of animal, if our method of determining intelligence by the convolutions of the brain is correct, yet he contradicts our decisions by doing work which is so clearly the result of reasoning power. It is all very well to say as Bennett did that " the intelligence of a beaver is recognised as nothing more than a remarkable instinct exerted upon one particular object, and upon that alone. In all respects, except as regards the skill with which he constructs his winter habitation, and the kind of combination into which he enters with his fellows for carrying their common purpose into effect, his intelligence is of the most limited description." Is this altogether fair ? Are we to judge an animal by what he is or by what he does ? I do not know whether Mr. Bennett ever visited the beaver in their wild state or simply obtained his information from the Zoological Gardens. The former seems scarcely possible or he would never have stated the two exceptions to the beavers' limited intelligence. The mere fact that animals work together does not prove any particular intelligence. Many of the lowest forms of animal life do that. Neither is the building of the winter habitation a work comparable with much that the beaver does as a proof of intelligence. It has often been cited against the beaver by those wishing to prove the animal's mental inferiority that when in captivity they do what are apparently senseless things, such as the cutting of chair-legs and unnecessary damming up of streams. There may be reason for these, as for instance, the sharpening of the teeth by cutting the wood. While in the latter case, it may simply be for something to do. Do we not do equally idiotic things when time hangs heavy on our hands ? Watch people sitting on a beach and see what many of them do. But we don't judge their intelligence by such ridiculous exhibitions. An animal as industrious as the beaver probably finds it difficult to refrain from some sort of activity. It does not seem fair to judge any animal except by the work he does and the method of doing it, for that is the way we judge ourselves. The actual fact of cutting down a tree does not necessarily, as already stated, show any very great intelligence, but the method employed frequently does. Take for example, the tree shown in the photograph. That tree was directly perpendicular, its branches resting slightly against the neighbouring trees. The beavers cut round it to a depth which would certainly cause it to fall if there was the least wind. To have cut more deeply into it would have been dangerous, as without warning the tree would have dropped straight down and caught the beaver's head in all probability. Presumably the animal understood this, judging from the fact that he left it. Fortunately, I obtained a photograph of the tree only a few hours before it fell, a slight breeze having caused it to overbalance.

Beavers' blazing or marking on a birch tree. Probably done to test the condition of the bark, to see whether it was ready for being cut and stored.

A most interesting example of beaver cutting. The tree was slightly supported by the branches of other trees so that it remained erect even though cut through so that the core was only half an inch in diameter. Had the animal made one more cut the tree would have dropped on its head, so it was left to be blown down by the first breeze.

This shows that second thoughts are best. To have continued cutting on the lower side would have been dangerous, so that it was abandoned and the work re-started on the upper and safer side. Note the tooth marks on the larger tree, a birch, thirty-two inches in diameter.

A beaver pond in North Ontario; showing how the course of a stream was diverted.

Another common example of their intelligence is shown by the way in which they will add water to a brook whose supply seems inadequate to their needs. They will turn other streams into the one which is failing them, by digging ditches to carry the water, by even diverting an entire stream towards their own, and by tapping springs by means of small ditches. Their comprehension of the entire problem of water supply and control is so altogether wonderful as to be almost incredible, and even so some people claim that they do not *reason*.

Numberless incidents of a more or less similar nature could be told to prove that by the *means* employed in doing the work the beaver reasons with the utmost clearness, while the results of their work justify us in believing that they thoroughly appreciate what are, or should be, the *ends*. Nothing proves this better than the building of the canals to which reference has already been made. These artificial waterways are apparently constructed with but one end in view: the simplifying of transporting cuttings of wood. Carrying and pushing logs and branches on land, whether through the tree-strewn and moss-covered forests, or over the hummocky grass lands, is a difficult and tedious task to be avoided whenever possible. But as the trees which are growing near the pond, whether natural or the result of beaver work, are cut down, the supply naturally recedes further and further with each season. To counteract this the beaver enlarge the dam, making it both longer and higher, so that a greater area is flooded. There comes a time, however, when a limit is reached, either through the natural conformation of the land or through the beaver's inability to build a dam beyond a certain height. They are then confronted with the problem of getting to and from the trees, on which they depend for food, without the necessity of travelling on land. By a very gradual method, which probably originated by the enlarging of small natural openings in the bank, the beaver worked out the canal scheme. When this happened no one can say, as the ditches very soon lose all trace of their origin, but there is every reason to believe that it has been going on for very many thousands of years. Where conditions are favourable canals reach the extraordinary length of upwards of 1,000 feet. Of course, this gigantic work is not all done at once, but gradually, as the supply of food trees goes back further and further from the pond. It might be presumed that these canals are only run through level country, but here is the greatest evidence of the engineering ability of the beaver: they build their canals uphill by means of weirs or dams, the distance between them varying according to the gradient. Yet they never work uphill unless it is made absolutely necessary by the contour of the land. They avoid hills just as carefully as man does when engaged on similar work, but when confronted with an unavoidable obstacle

in the form of rising ground they are not daunted.
If the canal is needed it must be made, and the
work is carried on with the fullest appreciation of
the water problem, so far as it concerns them. The
little dams which separate the different levels are
simple affairs, mostly made of the material excavated.
Their length depends on the conditions. In flat
land none are built, for they are not needed.
Where the rise is very slight they are only the
width of the canal, increasing according to conditions, so that in some places they are six or seven
times the width of the ditch. This presumably is
to prevent a sudden rush of water which might
cause injury to the entire system. The dams,
though quite simple, are strong enough to be used
as passage-ways ; the animals, swimming down the
canal, drag their burdens over the dams, which on
the upper side are but a few inches above the level
of the water.

The width of these canals is usually about three
feet, with a depth of from one to three feet, seldom
deeper except when small pools are made evidently
with the idea of providing a hiding place in the
event of danger. Burrows are also made in the
banks probably for the same purpose. Apparently
every contingency is considered, and little or
nothing left to chance. The direction of the canals
must necessarily be variable. Wherever conditions
are favourable they are as straight as though laid
out by human engineers, but when there is any

advantage to be gained by curves they make curves, in other words they follow the lines of least resistance, appreciating the fact that a straight line is the shortest distance between two points. When the canal leads from the pond across more or less level ground to an abrupt hillside which is well-wooded, they are not content with simply running their canal to this hill, but they frequently make branches on either side, these branches often extending several hundred feet so that the beaver are able to take their cuttings by way of the canals with the least possible effort. In making the canals the animals scoop out the earth with their hands and put most of it on the banks. If the ditch runs parallel to the hill or rising ground, most of the earth is placed on the lower bank so that it will not interfere with supply of surface water on which they largely depend for keeping the canals sufficiently deep. In the low lands there is seldom any difficulty in the matter of water, as the seepage naturally finds its way into the ditch, but in some cases the beaver are confronted with the scarcity of water and they resort to most ingenious methods for overcoming the difficulty. They will search the immediate vicinity for a stream however small, or a living spring. This they will tap by means of a narrow ditch which leads the water to the canal, another example of the animals' careful reasoning.

Besides these long and ambitious canals which were, I believe, first described by Morgan, and

which are not very frequently found, there is the
very common form found in most beaver colonies.
These really can be more properly termed waterways than canals, as they are in places which are
already more or less flooded, but which, owing to
the shallowness of the water, and the numerous
hummocks, or tussocks, are scarcely passable to the
beaver laden with poles or branches. They therefore cut a way through, tearing down the obstructions, and excavating the mud until there is a
sufficient depth of water to allow them to travel
without difficulty. Then another form of canal,
which has already been partly described, is the kind
which is made in order to ensure a short cut either
from one pond to another or across a neck of land
formed by a sharp bend in the stream or river, or
even across a promontory running into their pond.
Apparently they consider it worth the labour, and
it must be a serious undertaking to cut a canal of
considerable size in order to shorten the length of
their journeys.

As a rule the canal work is done before the
woodcutting operations are in full swing, so it
shows that they actually make fairly complete
preparation for what they know lies before them
and proves pretty conclusively that the wood-
cutting is not a work undertaken on the spur of the
moment. Everything points toward such a conclusion, the selection of a place where suitable wood
is abundant, the building of the dams, and finally,

the making of canals and roadways. Nothing seems to be lacking in the chain of evidence. And the animal that does all this wonderful work and exhibits such extraordinary intelligence, what is it like ? An inconspicuous creature which resembles something between a large rat and a squirrel, weighing up to sixty-five or seventy pounds, about forty-five inches long when fully grown. The tail is thick, flat and closely-covered on both sides with small modified scales. The ears are short, dark and round covered with incon- spicuous short hair, the front teeth are long, curved and extremely sharp and strong. The body is covered with thick fur and hair of a general dark brown running into chestnut and greys. The legs are short and the front feet are small and more like hands, while the hind ones are long, broad, and completely webbed, thoroughly adapted to the animals' aquatic habits. This gives a general idea of the beavers' appearance, a fuller description of which will be found in another chapter. In swimming only the hind feet are used, the great spread of which enables the animal to maintain a surprising speed whether at the surface, or below water, where it can stay for eight or nine minutes without fresh air. The tail is employed to a very limited extent, its principal use being as a rudder. I have never been able to make absolutely sure that it is employed as a propeller, though I have watched beaver swimming on every available

occasion.   What appears to happen is that the tail
is used in starting, to give the first impetus by
means of several quick side strokes, after which
under ordinary conditions it does not seem to
move.   When a sudden burst of speed is required
the tail again comes into play, but only with a few
strokes so far as I could judge.

CHAPTER II

In the foregoing pages, the work done by the beaver has been described with more or less thoroughness. It has perhaps proved dull reading, but seemed necessary in order that the habits of the animal should be more fully understood, and his tasks more completely appreciated. We shall now see something of the life of these busy creatures, and the best way will be to follow them through several consecutive years, seeing how they live, and plan, and work together.

We will imagine that it is spring, the dreary, monotonous winter has passed. The sun is warming the earth and awakening the plant world to life and activity, the rich mosses of the northern woods are becoming more green and beautiful, and the flowers are unfolding their petals to brighten the country and tempt the drowsy insects from their long sleep. Everywhere the creamy white flowers of the bunchberry are strewn like snow over the woodland ground. Everything is awake and happy. The beaver who have no young are leaving their dark lodges, and seeking summer quarters, for before them lies a season of ease and happiness and good living.

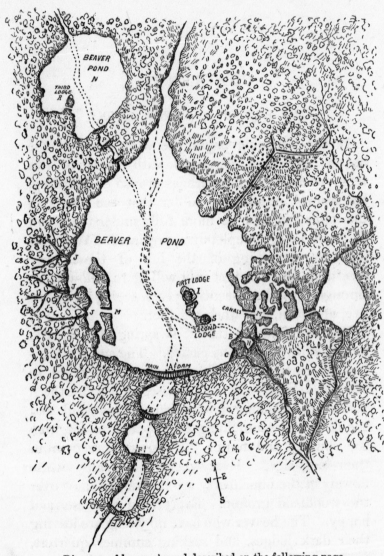

Diagram of beavers' pond described on the following page.

The streams shown in dotted line were dammed at A and B ; as the water rose it formed two other outlets, C and D. At these points additional dams were put. Later, to reinforce the principal structure, supporting or subsidiary dams, E, F, G and H, were built. On the island, I, formed by the rising water was the first lodge. On the west side are the roads, J, to the birch and maple trees. To the north-east is a canal, K, built in order that the beavers might have access to the grove of aspens, which was situated on rising ground and necessitated making the canal with three dams to hold the water at the different levels. Toward the end of the east wing of the canal is a straight line, L, indicating the small aqueduct or ditch cut by the beavers in order that water might be diverted from the streamlet to ensure an ample supply for the canal. Other small canals, M, are for the purpose of making short cuts when transporting food supplies. The upper pond, N, was made by the second pair of beavers, who had been driven from their own home by fire. The dam forming this pond is O, with subsidiaries P, Q. The lodge, R, on a point of land which has been formed into an island by cutting a ditch. The second lodge, S, was built by one of the young from the first lodge.

Let us choose an imaginary beaver, a young male, and follow him on what presumably would be his life. He is two years old and he has his way to make in the beaver world. No longer may he remain beneath the parental roof, for that is taxed to the limit of its capacity, and as his brothers and sisters have had to go off into the wilds to shift for themselves, so also must he. Two summers ago he was a mere kitten, dependent on his parents, too small to work, and without much knowledge. But the time has not been wasted. He has seen what work is required by those who would thrive, and he has helped in all the various labours. He has seen how dams should be built, trees felled, lodges made and repaired. He has, in fact, served his apprenticeship, and is now but little below full size, while his strength is equal to any demands that may be made upon it. But he is alone, and therefore incomplete. A helpmate is necessary if he would live up to the traditions of the race and found a colony, so he starts off from the pond which for two years has been his home, his playground and the scene of his labour. At first it is lonely work exploring new country, following one stream after another. One day he comes to a pond held captive by a large dam and he enters it, and swims toward a lodge which is on a small island. There is no one at home, or sign of any of his kind about. In vain he examines the shores for indications. The builders of the dam are gone, and the wood pile near the house tells the sad story. It has scarcely been touched since with infinite labour the little colonists had collected it for their winter food; the winter they would never know, for the steel trap had come to those peaceful woods, and had accomplished its deadly work. Silently each night by the side of the dam had it closed its relentless jaws on the beaver that had come to repair the unexplained break in the well-built structure. Each night saw the colony dwindle in numbers, until of the nine, old and young, but one remained, too frightened to venture out by day or by night, for fear of meeting the fate of the other members of the family whose death she had several times witnessed. She had been powerless to assist. She had seen her father and mother, her brothers and sisters suddenly clutched by the foot and dragged under water. She had dived down to see what it meant, and had seen them struggling at the bottom, trying in vain to break free from the iron thing and the heavy chain which had slid down the inclined pole. A few frantic efforts and the end came. No more bubbles rose to the surface, all was quiet again and there was one less beaver in the world. Not understanding the constant repetition of the tragedy, she was simply seized with fear, and she kept away from the place which seemed to be the cause of so much misery. Even when she saw, by the lowering of the water in the burrow entrances, that the pond was going down, she still stayed at home, going out only under water to the wood pile and quickly returning to the lodge with a small twig for her meal.

So she continued to live throughout the winter, escaping immediately the ice melted, and making her way among the patches of snow through the woods, but always following the course of the stream on which the pond had been made. She travelled slowly, sleeping during the day in holes in the banks. On her way she left signs here and there on conspicuous points of land. Small pieces of mud patted down and scented slightly with castoreum. Who shall explain her reason for doing this? Presumably it was meant as a means of communication with any other of her kind. If so it served its purpose, for the young male on finding the pond unoccupied, felt instinctively that there must be good reason for keeping clear of such an ill-omened place, and he slowly proceeded on his journey along the stream. For several days he continued on his leisurely way. At first there was no reason to hurry, but finally he came to one of the scented mud pats and became intensely interested. From it he learned that he was not alone. What more information he gathered from the inconspicuous pile of mud no one knows. But he too collected a small lump of mud and deposited it on the one he had found. Things looked different now. No longer did he dawdle along. He even threw caution to the winds and travelled by day, frequently finding fresher and fresher mud pats, until at last he overtook the maker of them. They met at night and beyond rubbing noses there was no formal introduction. They were both lonely and what more natural than that they should join forces to start out in life and travel together? The sealing of the life compact, which is seldom if ever broken by the beavers, was done without fuss or ceremony and was witnessed only by the moonlit trees.

The next question was where they should go? Not back to the deserted pond, for even though it would have meant a great saving of work, the fact that it was known to men made it a dangerous place to live. Far better would it be to find some quiet stream which was free from all taint of their persistent enemy. The whole of Northern Canada lay before them, but they were slow travellers, their short legs prevented long marches. They dared not go far by land, it would be too dangerous, as they had no means of defence, and could not escape by running away from even the slowest of their enemies. In the water alone had they any chance of safety. There they were in their element, and nothing could touch them save the "fire stick" which belched forth its tiny, deadly missiles, and killed at such great distances. And so they followed the stream until it brought them to a large lake. For some weeks they stayed there, roaming about as the fancy seized them.   The place offered great attractions to the house-hunting couple, and they were half inclined to settle there.   They even went so far as to commence building a lodge on a small wooded point which jutted out into the water. The two outlets to the lake they saw could be easily dammed if necessary, so everything, including an unlimited supply of wood, suggested the advisability of making this their home.   But one evening just as they had come out of a burrow near the foundations of their lodge, they were startled by a strange sound, human voices laughing and talking. Soon two queer objects came around the point of land, and the beavers saw two canoes ; the graceful lines of the dark green canvas-covered craft did not appeal to them.   What could they be ?   No such animals had they seen in all their travels, and so they lay immovable on the surface of the quiet water, and watched the canoes as they glided along. Closer and closer they came, when suddenly the air was tainted with the fearsome scent of man, that which above all things was most to be dreaded. Instinctively both of the silent watchers raised their tails and struck the water with a resounding smack which scattered the water high in the air, so that the countless drops reflecting the glorious colours of the setting sun resembled a golden shower. The beavers vanished beneath the disturbed water and sought safety in the dense tangle of brush with which the shore was lined, while the people in the

A beaver dam about 500 feet long but only 4½ feet in height.

Birch tree partly cut through by beaver.

canoe so suddenly startled by the noisy alarm
signal stopped, surprised to hear from the guides
that the terrific sound was made by beaver.

The party decided to camp near the place on
chance of seeing something of the animals about
which they had frequently heard so many remarkable stories. The guides, both of them being
trappers, made notes for future use. Yes, they
would come back in the proper season and get a few
beaver skins from that lake. But the beavers
thought differently. Their one idea now was to
escape as rapidly as possible from a place which had
proved to be known to man, and that night, while
the camp fires crackled in front of the tents, and the
sparks drifted lazily upward through the dark tree-
tops to be lost among the countless stars, the
beaver left their shelter, and under the cover of the
kindly starlight made their way to the further end
of the lake, where the outlet stream ran down
through the woods. Along this rocky waterway
they travelled, no word spoken, yet each filled with
the one idea of putting as great a distance as
possible between themselves and the human beings.
For a mile or two they followed this stream without
finding anything but rocks and steep banks.
Occasionally they stopped to nibble some particularly enticing twig, or to listen cautiously for the
possible approach of an enemy, but the woods were
wrapped in the stillness of night and almost the
only sounds were the murmuring of the brook as it

glided among the moss-covered stone, purring as it went, and far away the hollow who-who-who-whoo of the owl. Once they got the tell-tale scent of a silent-footed lynx, so they hid in the water for over an hour, till the air was cleared of the invisible warning.

Very early in the morning, when the sky was changing from the mysterious colour of night to the rosy hue which precedes the coming day, the beaver came to a little valley through which the stream flowed in a leisurely way. A tangle of alders marked a bog on one side and indicated the presence of a spring. On either side of the valley the sloping hills were well wooded with birches, poplars and maples, interspersed with spruces and pines. A little further along the stream divided into two branches, each finding its way from a different valley. The place attracted the beaver, but it was too near day for them to risk a careful and thorough investigation, so after making a hasty breakfast of roots and bark they sought the seclusion of an over-hanging bank where they could sleep comfortably and yet be near enough to the water to escape immediately if danger threatened.

The day passed slowly and no sooner had the setting sun thrown the shadows of the tree-covered hill across the grassy valley, than the beavers came out to examine the surroundings, and see whether conditions were favourable for making a home. Apparently, everything was to their satisfaction.

There were excellent sites for the two dams which would be necessary. Food was abundant, and from the appearance of the stream, they could count on an ample supply of water. They did not know that many years ago a small colony of beavers had lived there for several years, until a trapper had discovered their home and caught them all. That accounted for the grassy flat and for the division of the stream. In the many years which had passed since that tragedy the trees had grown again.

As it was too early in the year to attempt much work the prospective house-builders contented themselves with making a deep burrow in the bank, with the two entrances well under water. There they lived for several weeks, when the stream began to dwindle in size as the hot weather dried up many of the smaller tributaries. Then it was advisable to commence work on the dams, and with this object in view they cut a number of alders and laid them lengthways with the banks and across the shallow stream. More and more were added, with clumps of sod and mud worked in on the upper side, so that the flow of water was retarded. At the end of a week, a small pond began to form. This grew larger as the dams were made more solid. At first the large one was not more than twenty-five feet in length, but the engineers decided that if they wanted a pond of sufficient size the length must be extended, and so they built on to the structures until they were nearly doubled in size, and the pond increased correspondingly. With the deepening of the water, the beaver found their burrows were no longer dry, so they decided that it was time to commence building a lodge. Summer was now at its height, and autumn would be upon them soon after the next moon. So even though it was full early, they chose the site for the new house. The place decided on was a small alder-covered knoll which the rising water had surrounded and made into an island. It was close to a spring, which was of great advantage. The earth being fairly soft a burrow was easily made. It started under water and ended in the centre of the islet. All roots were cut off and the tunnel made quite smooth, with a diameter of about thirteen inches. Very few of the growing alders were cut, as for the present they would be of service in supporting the building. Later they could be cut if necessary.

These were busy nights for the little builders. Sticks of various sizes had to be cut and hauled up on the knoll ; some of the wood they collected from among the dead branches which had been floated by the rising water, others they cut and from these they often eat the bark. This reduced the amount of work necessary, as the cuttings thus served two purposes. No big trees were cut at this time, that would come later. Among the network of sticks they placed great quantities of fibrous mud and sod, which was torn from the bottom of the stream close

A lodge built on the bank of Sandy River (Newfoundland), with a large store of logs and brush piled in the water for winter use.

A beaver's road from the woods to the water.

Beaver short-cut path from pond to river shown in diagram.

to their island. That again served a two-fold purpose ; it made a deep place close to the house in which the winter food could be stored well below ice, and was the best of building material. The mud packed well among the woodwork, and the roots held it together and helped to prevent cracking. All this work was done with their hands, the clumps of sod being carried in their arms against the chin, and forced into position with the hands and nose. They did not follow the story-book method of patting it down with their tails. Very little mud was used in the centre of the lodge, as that was the ventilating flue.

The woodwork was laid apparently in a very haphazard way, but always with the idea of making a rounded dome of tangled material which could not easily be torn apart. With surprising speed this grew, and within two weeks it had reached a height of over three feet and a maximum circum-ference at the base of about twenty feet. The inside in the meantime had been cut out over the land entrance of the tunnel, leaving a domed cavity twenty-three inches high and four feet across. Even in its rough condition, the lodge was quite suitable for a summer home, but as a precautionary measure, a second tunnel was made to enable the inmates to escape rapidly in case of emergency, and they never could tell at what moment an otter might make his way in. They are unwelcome visitors and are so quick and strong that the beavers, notwithstanding their powerful teeth, are usually unable to cope with them. In water they are the only four-footed enemy that beavers dread. On land everything is different, for apparently the land is not their natural habitat.

Toward the end of August, the beavers were very comfortably settled, their pond was fully two hundred yards long and seventy or eighty wide. The supply of water brought down by the brook was sufficient for their needs, and they were engaged in cutting passages through the partly submerged grassy tussocks for the purpose of reaching the wooded shores with greater ease. Everything promised well when a prolonged spell of rain caused them great anxiety. The stream increased its volume until it was a raging torrent which swept all before it, clearing the banks of any debris that had been deposited by the spring floods. The dams, whose crests were many inches under the water, were threatened with complete destruction. Something must be done, and done soon, and the beavers did the only thing possible under the conditions. They tore open a great gap in the larger structure. It was a dangerous task, for the pressure of the water was terrific. However, by working carefully they succeeded in liberating an immense volume of water and so saved the dams. These were again repaired as soon as the flood subsided, when the entire work was not only strengthened but increased to a still greater height. so that it was nearly five feet at the highest point.   This necessitated a still further increase in length, with corresponding increase in the size and depth of the pond.   Fortunately their lodge had not been seriously injured by the unexpected rise of water.   The floor, it is true, had been submerged, which was quite natural, as it had been only four inches above the normal water level.   One thing leads to another, and the additional work on the dam meant that the floor of the lodge must also be raised, so they cut away part of the ceiling and used the material thus obtained for the flooring.   This in turn meant putting still more material on the outside of the house, as the thickness of the walls needed to be not less than three feet and the roofing a foot and a half, without the final coating of mud.

September with its cool clear days was in its last quarter by the time the young couple had everything in order.   The white frosts at night warned them of the approaching cold season for which full preparation must be made if they expected to live in comfort.   Most important of all the tasks was the food supply.   So they made a tour of investigation among the trees to see that they were in proper condition for being stored.   Several small birches were examined and partly cut in order that they should dry thoroughly before being felled.   They dry better and more rapidly while standing, so after the beaver had girdled them they went off to a small aspen grove and commenced serious harvesting. The trees were nearly a hundred yards from the edge of the pond on the further side of a piece of boggy thicket. So before any wood could be brought to the water a roadway had to be made. Part of this was really a canal which was cut straight through the swamp and from which all obstructions were carefully removed. When finished it was about three feet in width and a little over a foot deep. On shore the path was rather wider, and led directly from the end of the canal, to the centre of the grove where it forked so that three different paths gave access to the field of operations. This accomplished, the beaver began felling the trees. As each one dropped, and it took but an hour or so to bring down a tree six to eight inches in diameter, all the branches were neatly cut off close to the trunk ; these were carried down the road to the canal, the smaller ones being held, butt foremost, with the teeth, while the beaver either walked on all fours or only on his hind legs with the tail used as a balance. Some branches which were extra large were dragged along as the animal walked backwards until he reached the canal. From that point the work of transporting the wood became easier and he swam, leading the floating load with his teeth. In this way he proceeded through the canal then across the pond to the lodge near which they had decided to place the wood-pile. Sometimes, instead of immediately diving and taking the cutting to the bottom they would leave it floating

Beaver striking the water with his tail as a signal of alarm.   Both the head and tail are raised above water.

The end of the splash as the beaver disappears after sounding the signal of alarm.

close to the lodge, perhaps with the idea of allowing
it to become water-soaked, so that it could the more
easily be taken down. The journeys were quickly
made, and little or no time lost, except when
occasionally, on the return trip, they would stop
and take a short feed.

The trunks of the aspens were cut into convenient lengths varying from two to eight or ten
feet, according to the thickness. The shorter pieces
were rolled or pushed down the path, the longer
ones pulled, sometimes both animals working
together if the log happened to be unduly heavy,
using not only their hands and chests, but also
their hips. The entire operations proceeded
smoothly and with perfect system and in absolute
silence. Nothing was wasted and everything was
as tidy and orderly as possible. Interruptions
occurred at times when suspicious scents tainted
the air and caused them to suspect the proximity
of a foe. They would then scuttle off quietly to
the water and stay there so long as there was any
cause for alarm. Sometimes they dared not
approach the aspens for an entire night, owing to
the presence of wolves, foxes, or other predatory
creatures who consider beaver meat quite a luxury.
On these occasions they did not avail themselves
of the excuse to stop all work, for there was plenty
to be done. The dam could always take a little
more mud on the facing or more brush and logs
on the lower side, and the building of secondary

or supporting dams had to be considered. Who could tell but that the main structures might at any moment give way under the pressure of water, or the still greater pressure of broken ice, that enemy to all dams in the northern countries, whether built by man or beaver? Strong indeed must be the structure that will withstand its onslaught, when borne by the spring floods it hurls itself at every obstacle. Well-built bridges are smashed like matchwood, great trees are uprooted, banks are torn down, and ponderous boulders are swept before it, as creaking and groaning it grinds and forces its impetuous way in the company of the raging streams. The beaver, knowing the possibility of such an onslaught against their dams, whether by experience, instinct or reason, finally decided to erect smaller dams below the main structures. Owing to the narrowing of the gully it was only necessary that these dams should be very short, one near the larger outlet being twenty-five feet long the other fifteen, but as the ground sloped suddenly they had to be fairly high in proportion to their length. The work was carried on regularly and without difficulty, as there was very little water passing down the stream and building material was everywhere abundant.

Autumn stole upon the beavers while they were engaged on their many tasks. The days shortened, so that the increasing length of the nights gave them more working hours. The nights, too, were much colder, and the trees took on their wonderful clothing of scarlets and yellows. Those persons who have lived all their lives in the sombre east can have no idea of the glories of the western colouring. No pigment is richer or more brilliant than the leaves of these northern trees. The intense yellows of the birches and aspens, the scarlets, crimsons and oranges of the maples, and the endless array of purples and reds of the shrubs combine to make these woods a feast for the eye, beautiful beyond all power of description. It is the signal of the fall of the year, the advance guard of the long season of rest, silence and hardship, when the inhabitants of the wilds are hard pressed for food and the weakling and the improvident succumb under the great test of fitness. The survival of the fittest is the inexorable, pitiless law of nature which demands of her offspring perfection in power and resource. Those who are unable to battle against the frightful odds fall out of the ranks and are quickly forgotten by the survivors, the winners in the great race.

With the falling of the leaves the maples and birches which had been girdled or marked by the beaver a week or two earlier became ready for cutting, so the busy animals attacked them with their customary vigour and determination. It was not like felling the soft aspens, through whose tender wood their teeth bit with but slight oppo-

sition. These hard trees demanded far greater
effort, but the keen-edged teeth tore out the great
chips, and each night saw the fall of at least one
silvery birch or grey-coated maple, and the pile
of winter wood grew larger and larger till it
covered an area of full eighteen feet in diameter
and five feet in depth. It was hard work,
but it did not daunt the provident creatures,
who knew well enough that on the fruits of their
autumn labour must they depend for nearly half
a year, so the harvest was gathered without
murmur or complaint. Colder and still colder
were the nights, and by the end of October ice
formed around the margin of the pond and
wherever the water was sheltered; quite often
after dragging the cut branches down over the
carpet of crimson and gold leaves with which the
ground was covered the beavers had to break a
way through sharp-edged ice, and it warned them
that it was time they should attend to the outside
plastering of the house. This was a simple enough
job, but still it must be properly done. Not too
much mud should be put on at one time, but layer
after layer, pressed in firmly among the woodwork.
As each coating contracted under the influence of
the frost another coat was applied, so that gradually
the lodge assumed the appearance of a great mud
heap, which, as it froze, became stronger on the
outside and warmer in the cosy interior. At odd
times during this season they collected bedding

Lodge built among alders.

The ordinary type of dam found in a fairly flat district (Newfoundland).

Part of a poplar grove which was completely cut down by a small colony of beaver. It will be seen that the trunks are entirely stripped of their branches, which were carried away to the storage pile.

material. A little grass was cut and carried in, but grass gets wet and soggy and is not really a serviceable substance. Finely-shredded wood is better. So they cut down a cedar, which is the best of all trees for the purpose, and taking it piece by piece into the lodge tore it into fine shreds and made a deep bed, which was sanitary as well as comfortable. Of course certain parasites would make their home in it and cause the beaver great annoyance, but that could not be avoided. All they could do would be to use the curious split second toe-nail of their hind feet as a comb with which to make their daily toilet and dislodge the intruders.

As the home was nearing completion the beavers took in a pair of muskrats as uninvited tenants—for, curiously enough, muskrats nearly always make a winter home in the lodge, not living actually in the main room, I believe, but making a small nest for themselves in the wall, the entrance to which is either through an off-shoot of the regular burrows or else one made entirely by themselves. Apparently they do not interfere in any way with the rightful owners of the lodge, unless possibly they steal some of the smaller twigs from the wood-pile, for they too depend to some extent on bark for nourishment, though grass and roots form the greater part of their diet. Some writers maintain that the muskrat, or musquash, is an enemy of the beaver, who kill them whenever the opportunity occurs. This may be the case in some parts of the country, but I have never seen the slightest evidence of it. On the contrary, I have watched the muskrats going in and out of the lodges and working about the wood-pile while one or more beaver were there, and they paid not the least attention to their little cousins. So also when the beavers fell a tree into the water the muskrats will keep them close company while they are at work. I have seen the little fellows cut off small twigs from a birch tree from which two beavers were busily engaged in stripping bark and branches and carry it away to some hiding place unknown to me. Whether or not the muskrat does much damage to the dams is not apparent. They have their regular crossings over the tops of the dams, but I have never found any sign of damage which could be directly attributed to them. This, however, can scarcely be said to prove them innocent, because the experience of other observers does not altogether agree with mine. The mere fact that the beaver allow the muskrat to live unmolested in their lodges should at least be regarded as an indication of the seemingly friendly relations of the two. In both Newfoundland and Canada I have almost invariably noticed on approaching a lodge very quietly that at the vibration caused by my walking a muskrat will be seen slipping out from the lodge under water, a few bubbles rising to the surface as he swims near the bottom. At first I used to believe they were young beaver, but that idea was soon dissipated by the little fellows coming up close to where I lay concealed, when I could identify them without any doubt.

By the middle of November the lodge in which our pair of beaver lived was completely finished. It was smooth and tidy, with scarcely any sticks showing, nothing but mud, and roots, and a small amount of grass and sod used as an outside plastering. About this time the pond froze over completely except above the spring to which allusion has already been made. Only on very cold nights was there sometimes a thin layer of ice over this part, but even this usually melted during the day time. As winter settled down on the country, the beaver were seldom seen out of doors. Occasionally on a particularly warm sunny evening, one would come out through the spring hole and take a look over the house. But there was no work to be done, so the beaver resigned themselves to the long season of rest and inactivity, welcome, perhaps, after their two months or more of really arduous labour. One day was much like another. Having nothing better to do, they slept most of the time, coming out only for an occasional swim in the ice-covered pond or to get some twigs from the wood pile. These they would cut off in convenient lengths, take into the house and eat the bark. This done, the peeled stick would be carried out and left

the forest was broken by countless tons of moving ice which bounded along in the seething water, now piling up in great walls as some obstacle barred its path, then breaking loose and tearing all before it. The upper end of the beavers' pond was a mass of broken ice brought down by the stream. For some time it could not break its way through the solid sheet which covered the pond. Gradually the unceasing flow of water forced a passage through the dam where the ice again piled up as though impatient of the delay. During these days, the beaver frequently came out for an airing, often going into the woods in search of some fresh food. It was a dangerous undertaking, for their enemies were thin, hungry, and keenly alert, and the slightest prospect of beaver meat gave stimulus to their cunning. Several times during those first visits to the woods did the beavers escape by an all too-narrow margin, reaching the water only just in time to miss the white fangs of their quick-footed enemies.

By the end of March all trace of the winter's snow had vanished except in the darkest glades where the sun did not penetrate. Gradually, the first signs of spring became visible. Small green shoots appeared among the dead leaves and mosses, the buds on the trees began to swell and give promise of foliage, and by the middle of April the woods were tinged with the tenderest green of the new leaves. This was the most important period of the beavers' life. Already the female was becoming restless, making and remaking the bed of shredded wood and grass. She did not appear to care for the society of her mate, who kept away from her during much of the time. Finally he left the lodge, and sought a temporary home in a bank burrow, and it was but a few days later that in the lodge could be heard the faint whining cry of a newly arrived family of three. Three small, furry imitations of their parents, about twelve inches long and rather greyer in colour than they would be later; their ears were very dark and their eyes were open from the first day,* and their teeth good miniatures of those with which their parents had done so much useful work. Occasionally the young father came into the lodge, but he seldom stayed long, evidently he considered it wise to let the mother have the place to herself and young. For two weeks she kept them in the dark, warm house, nursing and watching over them with the true solicitude which is so wonderful and so exquisitely unselfish in what we term the lower forms of life. Willingly would she have sacrificed her own life if occasion demanded. No danger would have been considered too great if her offspring were in peril, but fortunately they were safe and she only had to nurse and caress them while they got their strength.

---

* Some authorities claim that the young are blind at birth, but the opinion of trappers and others with whom I have spoken is that their eyes are open from the first.—A. R. D.

In less than three weeks, they made their bow to the great outdoor world, swimming about without effort or fear, in evident enjoyment of the bright sunlight that was such a contrast to their dark home. A short swim sufficed for the first day, and one by one, of their own accord, they dived (without having to be taught as our fanciful writers would make us believe) and returned to their lodge to dry off and sleep after these first exertions.

The day and weeks that followed were filled with the joy of living. Spring flowers blossomed and passed to give way to later ones, the birds returned from their winter journeys in the balmy south, and filled the green-clad forests with their varied songs. It was their season of courtship and nest-building, all following the laws of their kind with a precision that no man can understand. At a certain time the home of each particular species would be completed, nor did they vary more than a few days from one year to another. What almanacs did they consult that they should be so exact? Yet had they not arrived, each species at its own exact time, all arrayed in their brightest dress, whether of yellow, blue or scarlet, or the more sombre hues, to stay in the northern land for a definite period and for a definite purpose? The young beavers played about to the music of the woodland birds, yet no one dare say that they paid the slightest attention even to that most exquisite of songsters, the hermit thrush, whose rich, full

notes sound like the call of some happy, peaceful
soul that has passed away to the land of shadow
and mystery. Amid such surroundings was it
ordained that they should live, knowing few cares
or troubles, spending the hours in happiness,
innocent as yet of the fear of man. They were
a playful trio, frolicking about in the water like
kittens on land, playing among the fluffy, wind-
blown willow seeds that raced across the water like
tufts of eider-down, or later among the broad
leaves of the spatter-dock and the water-lily,
filling the snowy petals of the flowers with spark-
ling drops as they splashed the water with their
diminutive tails. They played hide and seek, like
children, pushed each other off the half-submerged
logs exactly as boys would do, all the time gaining
the strength and agility which play is destined to
give. When the sun was shining they would often
sit on the banks of the pond and after making a
careful toilet indulge in the luxury of a sun bath,
sleeping, yet ever watchful. No one could say at
what moment during the day a silent-winged hawk
might swoop down on them, for they were small,
and tender enough to tempt the appetite of those
that feed on flesh. When a hawk is seen, even
though it appears as a speck in the heavens, the
little furry creatures will scramble into the water
and either resume their play or go into the lodge
for greater safety, usually giving a little, child-like
cry of alarm, and on entering the lodge they hold

an animated but very subdued conversation like the muffled whining of very young babies.

While still quite small the beaver took to solid food, nibbling the bark from thin, tender twigs, so that the process of weaning was very gradual. During the summer months they spent much of their time outdoors, frequently without their parents ; at the slightest suspicion of danger, they would slap the water with their tails in quaint imitation of their parents. The sound they produced was faint, but still loud enough to arouse the mother, who usually came out to see what threatened her little family and make them seek shelter either in the lodge, a burrow, or more frequently among the thick grass which lined the pond. When they were about two months old they took up their quarters for a time in a large burrow which had been made for the purpose, the lodge being left, probably for the annual spring cleaning, which simply means the destroying of the insect parasites (*platypsyllus castoris*), with which the bedding becomes more or less infested, but which is believed to be dependent on the living creature for its own existence.

Only too quickly the summer passed. The lowering skies and cooler nights foretold the coming of autumn. But the warm, bright weather had served its great purpose. The birds had given to the world a new population to take the place of those that had died or been killed. In the warm

The beavers' dining place shown by the peeled sticks.

The beavers' summer home. A hole in the bank.

Beaver cuttings, seven-eighths natural size. Of the four pieces on the left the largest is cedar, a soft wood, the other three birch. These are about the average size of cuttings; the shredded wood on the right is beaver bedding.

days, the young had grown and thrived on the vast insect life which abounds in those northern woods. The trees had flowered and fruited, that new seeds might be sown and young trees grown to fill the ranks of the old and fallen. Smaller plants had gladdened the woods with their minute spots of colour and furnished fruits and seeds to feed many creatures during the coming winter. The wild meadows were filled with new grasses to feed the deer and others that were dependent on such simple diet, and everything had gone along in its wonderful, orderly way, arranging supply and demand with supernatural accuracy, leaving the annual balance-sheet audited by the unseen power that takes charge of all our accounts, whether it be the tiny and apparently insignificant chickadee whose duty it is to protect the forests against the ravages of certain insects or man whose responsibilities are so far-reaching.

The young beaver family had thrived and grown, and were ready to assist their parents to the best of their small ability, and even if their help was of little account they could at least learn, by watching, how the various tasks were accomplished. Not intentionally did the parents undertake their education. That only happens in story-books in which the authors try to humanise the animals and make them follow our own further advanced and complicated methods which change as our lives become more and more complex. The animals have a very marked inherited instinct to follow in the footsteps of their predecessors which causes them to do things naturally. We think that we teach a child to walk, but if we made no effort to do so the child would naturally walk because of the inherited tendency to do that which has been done by ages of ancestors. As the beavers swam, dived and fed without being taught, so also did they cut wood with their teeth without having to be shown how to do it. By observing the work of their parents they undoubtedly acquired a greater knowledge of how things could be done with the least effort and best results. Whether they knew *why* trees were cut, branches stored, lodges and dams built before they had experienced the rigours of winter, we cannot say, for we do not even know definitely how animals impart knowledge and exchange ideas.

By the time that occasional spots of scarlet pointed out the earliest of the maples, and the migrating birds had started southward, the beavers began seriously to repair the dams; fresh material was added, and the height and length slightly increased, the lodge also needed material, as the heavy rains had washed away much of the earth-work. The branches which had been peeled during the winter for food were now utilised in the various repair works. Even the inside of the lodge required attention as it was rather small for the increased family, so a little excavating was done until it was large enough to accommodate the five occupants. Another entrance was also made in case of emergencies. Tree cutting began as on the previous year as the colouring of the trees was passing its prime. But now they needed a much larger supply of winter food as there were more than twice as many mouths to feed and none of the supply gathered a year ago was now fit for food. Some of it was dragged on to the house and dam, but most was left to anchor the fresh cuttings, and to form an arched way to the newly made tunnel. While all these tasks were being accomplished, the young beaver followed their parents, sometimes biting down very small shrubs and carrying twigs to the food pile. They even brought up little clumps of mud and put them on the lodge and dam. From one task to another they went like restless children, always busy doing something or nothing. They had almost completely given up coming out during the day time, and seldom appeared until an hour before the sun had vanished behind the trees.

Toward the middle of November, the first flakes of fluffy snow drifted slowly and aimlessly down on the frozen earth. It was the advance guard of the storms which would soon follow. Very gradually the white mantle spread, and the soft browns, greys and greens of the land were hidden and the beavers snuggled down in their cosy warm beds, contented and confident that winter with all its hardships had

no terror for them. Their house answered their
every purpose, while outside, enclosed securely
beneath the ever thickening ice, was their harvest
of wood : maple and birch and ash and poplar, and
many other kinds, forming altogether a diet sufficiently varied to satisfy the most fastidious of
beavers.   Here in their well-planned home we may
leave them for the long winter, during which time
they grow fat and live a lazy life.   With the
coming of spring, the father beaver was once more
requested to leave his home for a new family was
expected.   He took up his quarters in the burrow
where they had all lived during part of the summer.
On coming into the lodge one day toward the end
of April, he was welcomed by the tiny whimpering
of four newly-arrived kittens, exact duplicates of
those that had come just a year before. The
founding of the new colony seemed well assured
now that instead of two there would be nine to do
the various works.   Of course it meant an increased
drain on the food resources of the neighbourhood,
which was none too abundant in the immediate
vicinity of the pond.   During the weeks following
the arrival of the new family, the father beaver
spent much time wandering about as though making
plans for the future.   Perhaps he realised that the
food trees were becoming somewhat scarcer near
the water, and that harvesting for the coming
autumn would involve a lot of very hard work.
This would seem to have been his course of reason-

A large birch tree very clumsily cut.

Beaver cutting up a birch branch.

ing, though there is no proof, and perhaps the extended wanderings were simply the result of restlessness after long months of inactivity. Within a distance of several hundred yards all around the pond his journeys took him and little escaped his keen eye. Among other things he noted to the eastward of where the short canal had been cut that there was a small knoll on which there was a dense growth of aspens whose silvery leaves trembled incessantly in the slightest breeze ; a very promising supply of food it was, but unfortunately it would mean a long, difficult portage of nearly two hundred yards, all over rough ground. He stored this information away in his brain, but did not avail himself of it for many weeks, during which time he made frequent trips, chiefly down the main stream, stopping here and there to place a small mud pie signal so that other strolling beaver would know he had been there. Sometimes he was accompanied by one or more of his year-old children, but Mrs. Beaver stayed at home to look after her young ones, who were thriving as all healthy wild creatures do. During the late afternoons she would lie on the surface of the water and watch the youngsters playing. It was scarcely safe to leave them entirely alone as they often became so engrossed in their games that they would have fallen easy victims to any enemy. One day she left them for a few minutes, going under water in search of some dainty morsel of food. As she rose to the surface her quick eye caught sight of a goshawk flying low toward her young who were sunning themselves on the bank, utterly oblivious to the impending danger. Quick as a flash she gave a slight cry and struck the water with her large heavy tail. Instantly the four baby beavers made a rush for the water. The warning was too late, however, for the goshawk, like a flash of lightning, swooped down and caught one of the wretched creatures, not stopping in its powerful flight, but carrying its prey into the woods where it was lost to view. Like most of the tragedies of the wilds, it had happened quickly, and with scarcely any disturbance. The mother beaver took her three remaining young into the lodge, where she remained for a few minutes; then she came out quietly, and after making sure that all was safe, swam slowly to where the four kittens had been sunning themselves so peacefully only a short time before. On landing, she nosed about until her nostrils found the scent of her lost one and the hawk. She raised herself up, sitting on her hind legs with her small hands hanging by her side and gazed wistfully toward the woods which had swallowed the little kitten. A low cry escaped her lips, but no answer was returned. Again she repeated it without result, her nostrils quivering all the time as though trying to get the faintest hopeful scent. In her heart she well knew that she would never see the one she sought again, yet the hopefulness of despair com-

pelled her to utter the mother's call. It was all
over, the lesson was learned, both by herself and
her family, and she swam back, diving without
noise, and disappeared in the lodge where three
frightened and hungry kittens awaited her.

Fortunately no other misfortune marred the
happiness of the little colony during the summer.
The weeks were spent in play and enjoyment and
in investigating the surrounding country. Shortly
before the approach of autumn the plans which had
probably been formed many weeks earlier took
form. The aspen grove must be reached and it
was decided that the old canal should be extended
from the part which had been started the previous
year to where the trees grew. Excavating a suitable trench was not easy work, but the two old
beavers, with the assistance of their three well-
grown children, undertook the task. The canal
started at the lake. It was about two and a half
feet wide and fifteen inches deep. Some of the
mud was taken out and carried into the pond, but
most was piled up on the sides. It ran in a direct
line toward the aspens, but after it had extended
about seventy yards, the rising land made it
necessary to dig down to a depth of two feet or
more in order to have sufficient water. Evidently
they could not continue in this way, as it would
mean making a trench over four feet deep before
the desired end could be reached, so the intelligent
animals constructed a small dam and continued the

ditch at a higher level. Two more such dams were found necessary, each raising the water to the proper level. On reaching the foot of the knoll on which the aspens grew, the canal was divided into two wings, but in these there was a lack of water which made them almost useless except during wet weather. The father beaver remembered having seen a tiny stream which flowed not far from the end of the longer wing, and, taking advantage of this, he cut a narrow ditch only a few inches wide and diverted some of the water from the streamlet to the canal, so that it had sufficient for its purpose. It was a clever piece of work and showed well how highly developed is the engineering skill of the beaver.

The weeks passed with alarming rapidity while this great task was being accomplished, and though the animals worked literally tooth and nail, they had to bestir themselves in order that everything might be in order before winter set in. A considerable amount of work was necessary on the dams, not only in repairing the original structures, but in extending them once more so that the size of the pond could be slightly increased. Then also the lodge needed material enlargement in order that the eight beavers might be able to live comfortably. It was altogether an extremely busy autumn and all hands worked with a will, apparently without any supervision, each doing what he or she considered most necessary. By the time

Beaver's lodge which has received part of its winter coat of mud and sod.   In front of it, in the water, is the store of winter food.

Three poplars cut from a single stump. Above them is the top of another tree which is being cut into length ready for transportation.

the leaves began to fall and carpet the earth with their varied and brilliant colours, but little harvesting had been done. Perhaps they knew that aspens are easily cut and that far more material could be gathered in a given space of time than if large tough-wooded birches and maples were to furnish the supply. However that may be, the cutting of the aspens did not begin in earnest until November. Then, as though suddenly realising the lateness of the season, a vigorous attack was made on them. Over a dozen were felled in a single night. Each one was quickly stripped of its branches and cut into convenient lengths and in this way carried down piece by piece to the canal and through it floated down to the pond and then to the wood pile. In going down the canal, each piece of wood was lifted over the dams, which soon showed much sign of hard wear, so that constant repairs were necessary. The year and a half old beavers did nearly as much work as their parents, and for nights there was an almost constant procession coming and going between the lodge and the head of the canal. With astonishing rapidity the store grew, and it would have been difficult to estimate the number of cords of wood it contained. Even during the freezing nights, when ice formed on the still waters, the beaver continued their harvesting, frequently having to break the ice which formed along the canal. Finally, one evening, they came out of the lodge to find their canal useless. Over half an inch of clear, "black" ice had formed over its entire length and they could not break it. So the aspen grove, or what was left of it, was abandoned, the smooth, gleaming white stumps bearing silent testimony to the remarkable activity of the beaver. The season of work was practically at an end. Here and there they managed to find a tree within their reach, but only where the streams ran into the pond and so kept the ice from forming could they bring any supplies. Around the lodge and wood-pile the ice was solid, except the region of the spring where but little formed, so that whatever branches were brought had to be transported for a considerable distance under water. When they finally rested from their labours the store was ample for their needs, even though winter should last beyond its usual time.

The months that followed were in no way different from those of the previous winter. But when spring came, instead of the father beaver leaving the lodge alone, he took with him his three older children, and lived with them in the summer burrow. The mother, who later gave birth to four kittens, lived in the lodge with the three survivors of the previous year. This season a change was decided upon. The family, now numbering twelve, would crowd the lodge beyond its capacity, so the three older ones were given to understand by their parents that they must seek homes for themselves. One went off alone to see the world, and as he never returned it is likely that he either found a mate who, like himself, was a wanderer, or else he joined another colony. Fortune was kind to his two sisters, who for the moment wished to remain in the vicinity of the parental pond. A small family which had its home a couple of miles further down the stream had met with disaster. Fire, that most terrible of all foes, had carved its deadly way around their pond, leaving a charred and blackened mass where all had been so green and alive. Their food supply gone, they had been forced to abandon the house which had sheltered them for two happy years. One road was as good as another, and it happened that they came along the stream on which our beaver lived. While journeying along, they came to some of the little mud-pat signals made by our beaver. What those silent signals told them no man knows, but they came on with renewed hope, and one day arrived at the pond we have been watching. There were four of them, an old pair and two young males, their children. Their presence was soon known to the resident colony, but there was not much in the way of introductions. Sufficient for them that they were accepted as friends, and allowed to remain for the present at least. As might naturally have been expected, the two young males decided to take unto themselves the two young females as wives, and one of these new pairs, delighting in their freedom and independence, went away to some new part of the country and began housekeeping according to their own ideas. They were mated for life and therefore it was only right that they should select some place which would allow the starting of a new colony, with ample room for expansion. Their decision was wise, for had they remained the pond would have been somewhat overcrowded, and that is quite contrary to the rules and regulations of beaverdom. Everything is regulated from the point of food supply, and so according to the resources of the neighbourhood must the growing of a colony be limited. The young pair that remained decided to build their lodge on the little island on which the original one was placed, but a dividing ditch was cut so that each lodge was on its own individual island. The older pair of visitors, not considering it wise to encroach too much on the hospitality of their new friends, made a pond for themselves by damming the smaller stream that flowed into the lake and which had originally joined the main stream. In their newly made pond they arranged to build a lodge on a point of land which they severed from the shore by cutting a broad channel. This seemed an almost unnecessary waste of labour if it was intended as a means of protection, for any animal large enough to be regarded as an enemy could easily jump across. It might, however, prevent tunnels being made from the land which would allow of access to the interior of the lodge.

During the summer, the beavers wandered about the country and were seldom much at home, but towards the middle of August they returned for good, and slowly did what work was necessary in the way of building and repairing dams and lodges. The older pair of visitors kept pretty well to their own pond, building their dams and lodge without assistance from the rest of the colony, who had quite enough to do to attend to their own needs. When wood harvesting began, the two families in the larger pond made a single wood-pile which would serve them both. With eleven mouths to feed it was necessary that the store should be even larger than on the previous year. Most of the harvesting was obtained from the aspen grove at the head of the canal, and the number of trees cut was past all belief. The woods resembled the scene of serious logging operations as carried on by men. Paths were cut intersecting the whole knoll and everything was most orderly ; each stump was a triumph in the art of wood-cutting, clean and smooth as though cut by an experienced lumber-man. No waste was to be found anywhere. Every trunk whose bark was in proper condition was neatly divided into convenient-sized sections and removed to the wood-pile, not even a twig was left. Besides the aspens, the beaver occasionally undertook the more laborious task of cutting

down large birches, the bark of which has a very
different flavour. These birches, growing as they
did among the older trees, often presented difficult
problems. One large one in particular, which had
a very heavy top of branches, was cut after many
nights of hard work. Unfortunately it lodged in
a neighbouring birch and would not fall. Another
cutting was decided on and continued until the
twenty-two inches (diameter) had been gnawed
through. But even this did not accomplish its
purpose, for, though the trunk shifted a few feet,
the top remained entangled. The tree against
which it rested in such an aggravating way was
nearly as large as the one that had been cut, but
even that did not daunt the little wood-cutters,
who went to work with renewed determination to
cut through its massive trunk. By the third night
they had cut most of the way through, but the
trunk, creaking with the great weight of the tree
which leaned against it, filled the beaver with fear,
for should it fall there was great danger of being
caught beneath the mass of branches. So they
left the task unfinished, perhaps hoping that the
two trees would fall of their own accord.

Fortune favoured them, when a few nights later
a violent storm swept over the country, the roaring
winds screeched through the forest, snapping off
branches and uprooting many large trees. The
winds lashed the water of the lake into a mass of
foam, threatening even to tear the wood-pile away

Beavers' road from the water to a grove of poplars.   All obstructions are
removed so that branches and logs may be brought to the water with
the least possible effort.

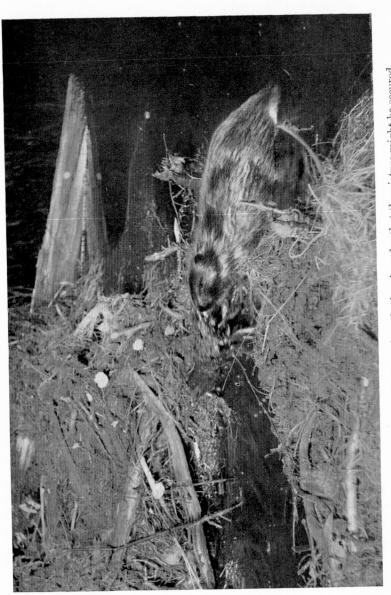

Beaver inspecting the dam which has been broken in order that the picture might be secured.

from its moorings. For two days and two nights the gale raged without a pause, and during that time the beavers kept in their lodges, for well they knew the dangers of falling timber. At last the storm passed, and the roaring of the wind and creaking of the trees gave place once more to the wonderful, overpowering stillness of the forest lands. Once more the pond reflected the beauties of the encircling woods. But a great change had taken place in the appearance of the country. Before the storm, the forest was a parti-coloured mass of dark green, golden yellow, orange and scarlet, a shimmering kaleidoscope of colour, but the ramping wind had stripped the branches of their gorgeous coverings, and left the woods a sombre symphony of greys and greens, while the ground was strewn with wind-blown wreaths of brilliant leaves.

When the beaver came out to see what damage had been done, they found that the lapping water had torn away the upper side of one of the lodges and carried off many large poles that had been laid on the roof. The dam, too, had suffered, and would need countless handfuls of mud to take the place of what had been washed away. A visit to the canal showed how that too had been damaged. Trees growing along its banks had been uprooted and the ditch was made impassable by the fallen branches and *débris*. True enough, they would find much material among the windfalls that could be utilised, but the work of clearing the canal was serious and occupied many nights. During this time they had been too busy to visit the lodged birch and its partly-cut neighbour. But at last one of the older beaver went ashore, probably with the idea of seeing what had happened, and he had the satisfaction of finding both the trees lying on the ground in a confused mass. Here indeed was a harvest which was worth considering, and forthwith he began cutting off a branch, which he immediately carried down the mossy bank to the water and across the pond to the wood-pile. One of the other beaver, seeing him come so heavily laden, surmised the truth and followed him back to the source of such richness, while she in turn was soon followed by several others. Before doing much cutting, however, they decided to make a better road, as there would be a very great number of loads to be carried. A direct course was therefore chosen from the fallen trees to the nearest water. In a couple of hours this was finished, for all worked together with but one end in view. No foreman directed their efforts, each individual seemed to know exactly what was needed, and each did what was necessary without the slightest instruction or advice, and therein is one of the great mysteries of beaver work. How is it they work in complete concert and harmony even when engaged in most difficult undertakings ? No plans are drawn, no orders given so far as we know, and yet the work is carried on as smoothly as though done by a body of skilful artisans under the instruction of a trained foreman who in turn receives his orders from a competent engineer.

The first thing to do after making the path was to cut off the outer branches which lay on the ground. This alone occupied two nights. Then, by climbing along the leaning trunks, all the larger branches were neatly bitten off so that the trunks, relieved of their support, came gradually to earth and were divided into lengths varying according to the diameter ; nothing over eight inches through being carried away. But even the thickest parts of the trunk that had to be left were not wasted, for the beaver ate all the bark which was suitable for food. It was noticeable that the two old beavers in the upper pond took no part in cutting up these trees. Their colony was entirely separate, and they must do all their own cutting. In other words, poaching was not allowed. In about ten days, nothing remained of the two tall trees but the stumps, two lengths of partly peeled trunks and a mass of large and small chips that were beaten into the well-trampled ground, these and the scarred pathway to the water, and the greatly-augmented wood-pile.

From that time up to the freezing of the pond the usual preparations for cold weather were carried on, so that when the pond froze and the country received its winter winding-sheet everything was in readiness. The lodges had been plastered, bedding gathered, the dams thoroughly overhauled, and the outdoor store-house a credit to the foresight of the little caterers.

The winter passed without excitement. During January, a few days of unusually mild weather produced a great thaw, so that the ice, weighted down by the melting snow, broke away from the shores. The beavers took advantage of this, and came out to bask in the cold sunshine. Some climbed on the lodges, while others more adventurous in spirit went ashore, their broad, deep trails marking their short journeys to the woods. Besides this little holiday no other event broke the monotony of the long imprisonment. At last came the welcome death of winter, and the gradual arrival of spring which saw the colony increased by no less than twelve new arrivals. The founders of the colony boasted of a fine family of five new kittens. In the lodge next to them there were three, while the pair in the upper pond had four, and all these families were born within a period of two weeks. The colony might now be said to be in a flourishing condition, with a population of twenty-five, where less than five years before there had been but two. Unfortunately, such prosperity was not destined to continue, or we might have seen the colony double itself by the following spring. That would have meant the facing of new problems in the way of expansion, for even after allowing the departure of two or three pairs, which would certainly have occurred, the remaining forty or fifty would have made great inroads into the food supply. The old dams would have to be enlarged and new ones built so that a larger area might be flooded. The canals would have to be extended and in every way great changes would be bound to take place.

During the month of July, when the whole country was throbbing with life and activity, when everything presented such a marked contrast to the four sombre months of winter, the unwelcome sound of man's voice broke the peacefulness of the little pond in the woods. A fisherman, anxious to explore the stream in hopes of finding a good place for trout, had come down from the lake above. With him was an old guide who lived, as so many of them do, by guiding fishermen during the summer, and big game hunters in the autumn, while the winter, or at least the early part of it, is devoted to trapping, the other part being often spent in lumber camps. It was late in the afternoon when these two intruders arrived. The beavers, lulled into a dangerous security by the long period of absolute God-given peace, were playing about the pond, the young indulging in their games with all the joy of youth and inexperience. On one of the lodges lay the founders of the colony, basking in the warm yellow sun, when suddenly the sound of voices reached their ears, followed almost immediately by the tainted breeze. No second warning was necessary. Silently the two slid off the lodge, but no sooner had they reached the water than each struck it a resounding smack that sent up a shower of sun-kissed drops. The command to dive was imperative, and every beaver in that pond and the upper one vanished instantly, and without a sound, to meet later in several of the burrows which had been made along the shore. The fisherman was much interested in the scene ; but he was after fish, not beaver, and he would far rather have seen the surface of the pond broken by rising trout. Had he but known it, that water contained many fine fish that had come down from the upper lake to enjoy the rich food in the beaver pond. The trapper saw the prospect from an entirely different point of view. Here was a thriving colony of beavers that represented perhaps a hundred and fifty or two hundred dollars to him. He walked round the pond, noted the size of the chips which indicated well-grown beavers, and, what was of great importance, no one had been before him. He would keep the news of the lucky find to himself, and as soon as the shooting season had passed, he would come armed with the deadly trap to destroy the colony that was engaged in a great, far-reaching work that he did not understand. Comparing the beaver and the man, we might well ask which was doing the greater good. The one bent only on destruction, while the other, though so insignificant, was devoting his entire energies to conserving, to doing that which, strangely enough, would be of

A dam made chiefly of large logs, the size of which is shown by comparison with man.

The same dam as that shown in previous illustration, photographed from the lower side; the man, who is over 6 feet tall, gives an idea of the size of the structure.

greatest benefit to the race which was for ever seeking his extermination—surely an ironical fate, and one that seems lacking in the elements of justice.

It happened that the trapper, though wise in his own way, committed a great mistake in making such a very thorough examination of the beaver ponds. He had frightened the occupants, which is not a wise thing to do, even during the summer, when the season for trapping is so far away. Many years ago, the pair of old beavers that had made their home in the upper pond after having been made welcome by the new colony, had passed through some very bitter experiences. They had seen a whole community wiped out of existence by trappers, and had been the only ones to escape. Again, two years later they had been ruthlessly pursued by human enemies and had seen all their offspring caught by the cruel steel traps. The presence of man to them was a very real danger which must at all costs be avoided. The security of the new home was evidently gone and the only thing left for them if they wished to live was to find another stream as far away as possible. They said nothing about their decision, but the old father took himself off quietly one fine night and for several weeks the colony did not see him again. He was intent on finding a suitable place in which a new colony might be founded and he journeyed many weary miles, often crossing thickly wooded hills in his endeavour to discover the desired stream. At length his efforts were rewarded, a small stream was found running between some rough hills which many years ago had been swept by fire. All the large timber had been destroyed and only the gaunt grey stumps remained as the gravestones of the magnificent forest. Surrounding them was a thick second growth of aspens, birches, wild cherries and maples which sheltered the ground and gave the seedling conifers a chance to make their start in life. Throughout this burnt land wherever an opening occurred, the ground was blazing with the brilliant magenta fire-weed. The conditions were most favourable for a beaver colony, for though the stream was small, it was fed largely by springs issuing from the rugged hills, and the food supply was sufficient for quite a large community. Satisfied with his investigations, the old beaver returned by a direct route to his home, guided by the sense which is possessed by animals, but which we do not understand; his arrival caused not the slightest surprise.

What happened during the days following no man can tell, but presumably he in some way made known his ideas as to the advisability of a general exodus, and most of the beavers considered his arguments sound. At least so it appeared if we may judge from what took place. For the colony, with the exception of the pair and their young which lived in the smaller house, abandoned the pond that had been the scene of such activities during the past five years. Under the leadership of the old beaver they trekked across country to the new land of promise. It was not a conspicuous band of immigrants that undertook the big journey, for they did not march all together, but in a long, straggling line, following each other by the invisible trail of scent as surely and easily as man follows his well-built roads. Travelling on land shows a beaver at his worst; he is slow, and even clumsy, and is at the mercy of any passing enemy. It is therefore with a feeling of dread that they venture far from water, so well do they realise their own shortcomings. Of the twenty-five that started out, only eighteen reached their destination. And it was only by good fortune that the death list had not been far greater. A pair of wolves out hunting for their cubs' dinner came across the beavers' trail. They needed no urging, for they knew that it was the trail of the most easily killed of all the animals in the woods. So they followed at a swinging trot, careful only to see that they did not overrun their quarry. Less than an hour later, the rising moon lightened up the tragedy, the details of which are quite unnecessary. Sufficient is it to say that seven beavers ceased to be, and had it not been for a small pond into which the others escaped, it is likely that the new colony would never have been founded. The wolves would have killed the entire band without the slightest difficulty. As it was, the survivors remained hidden in the pond all that night and the following day, and then, filled with fear lest their enemies might return, they hastened forward toward their destination, which was reached without further mishap. Then came the question of whether it would be better to make one pond and all live together in two houses, or whether two separate ponds should be made. The stream was small and the contour of the land did not offer facilities for making a large pond as the valley was narrow. So after careful investigation they made two narrow, long ponds within a few hundred yards of each other. The lower one received an additional supply of water from a second stream which joined the main one about a hundred yards above the place where they decided to put the dam.

It is unnecessary to relate how they carried on all the work for the new colony, as the methods differed in no essential way from what has already been told. The same sort of dams were built, except that more stone was used and more dry wood. The supply of mud being very limited, owing to the rapidity of the stream, the dam was largely filled in with sod, clumps weighing fifteen or twenty pounds being dragged into position. Two lodges were built, one in each pond. Six beavers lived in the upper lodge and twelve in the lower one. The entire work was completed before the cold weather began, and we may well leave them for the time to enjoy their hard-earned rest in the peaceful security of the new home while we return to the old pond to see what happens to those who would not give up their home and take the advice of their elders.

The shooting season having ended Joe, as we will call the trapper, returned to his little log cabin, satisfied at having been instrumental in the death of at least two unusually large moose (several others having escaped wounded) which he had called with his fatal birch bark horn until they were within easy range of the waiting sportsman. His thoughts now turned to the beaver colony which had so thoroughly excited his cupidity. From the walls of his shack he took down a bundle of carefully greased steel traps and examined them to see that all were in perfect order. Then he made a pack of a small tent, blankets, and some grub, and the inevitable kettle and pan, axe and rifle. Placing these on his back, with the weight hanging from his forehead by means of a tump line, he started out, filled with a keen sense of satisfaction, for he did not doubt the success of his undertaking, and a dozen or two of beaver pelts would make a very good start for the winter's work. Three days' hard travelling through the bleak autumn woods brought him to the pond which a few months before he had seen under such entirely different conditions. He approached carefully and made his little camp some distance from the lower side of the pond, so that no scent of man should alarm the unsuspicious beaver. Early the following morning he took several traps and set them in different positions, one being placed at each dam near a breach which he made, for he knew full well that the beavers are most careful to inspect the dams every night during the autumn and they would promptly mend any break they found. As he proceeded with his occupation his practical eye noted many signs of a most disturbing nature. Only one lodge had received its winter coat of mud, the wood-pile, and there was only one, was far smaller than it should have been. The dams in the upper pond were in bad condition and showed no evidence of having been repaired for many months, neither were there any fresh cuttings in or near that pond. More and more did Joe's hopes droop. That there were beaver in the place could not be doubted, as quite freshly peeled sticks were strewn along the shore and fresh browse projected above the water near the lowest house, but he was forced to the conclusion that the colony was far smaller than when he had seen it before. Had someone been before him and taken *his* beaver? In vain he searched for any indications of trap or man. Perhaps some wandering Ojibway Indian had visited the place and shot the beavers earlier in the season. Whatever the cause he felt disturbed. He had refused to join a friend on a trip to a region which promised rich returns in pelts because he had been certain in his mind that this pond would yield abundant profit for the amount of time and labour. Stump after stump he examined and all told the same story, if teeth marks could be relied upon. Two, probably, three-year-old beaver of medium size and some worthless youngsters. Truly a fine prospect for an experienced trapper! Strangely enough it had never occurred to him that the beaver might have taken alarm at his summer visit and moved to new quarters. He blamed the Indian and cursed him beneath his breath as an interloper and a thief who had stolen what he considered rightfully belonged to him. His disgust only increased when the following morning on visiting his traps he found two dead beaver kittens whose immature skins were almost worthless. For several nights after that he had no luck at all. In vain did he try his most cherished " medicine " made up of a secret compound of castoreum and other potent ingredients whose name he would not divulge to any living person, as they had been given to him many years ago by a dying companion who had been famous for his success in trapping. It was not until more than a week had passed that Joe caught one of the older beavers. Another of the kittens had also fallen a victim to his efforts, so that only one old one remained alive. In the end he too got into one of the carefully set traps, but fortunately the jaws had closed only on one front foot, and that was all Joe found in the trap when he came the following morning. The beaver had escaped, crippled and frightened, and Joe knew that further efforts to capture him would be useless, so in utter disgust he left the pond which had promised so much and given so little.

The three-footed beaver remained in his lonely home throughout the winter, leaving it as soon as the ice melted. What became of him after that is not known, but if we believe the stories of Indians and others whose lives are spent in the wilds he remained a lonely widower for the rest of his life, wandering about and living in burrows without sufficient ambition to build another lodge. This is a pretty fancy which, though not absolutely proven, has much to warrant its truth, and it shows the humble beaver in a delightful way, constant to but one wife whose memory is held sacred, if such a word may be allowed when speaking of animals. Everything in the beaver's life points to a fine moral nature. Their code of living seems high, and they live up to it in most cases. Some people deny to animals the knowledge of right and wrong, and by so doing prove how little they know of the subject. From the smallest bird to the highest form of mammal the sense of right and wrong is distinctly evident. How far it is developed we can only surmise. For almost the only opportunity we have of studying it is in our own relations with them, while when they are in their wild and natural state we know next to nothing of the intimacy of their lives. It is sometimes said that it is our influence that has developed in dogs their sense of shame at doing anything which they know to be wrong, and that it is not actual shame so much as fear of punishment which actuates their behaviour. To a certain extent this may be true, but what about the wild animals which punish offenders who are guilty of violating the laws of the pack or the herd ? If they had no sense of right or wrong this would never happen, for punishment of one creature by another can only result from a knowledge that wrong has been done, and with the realisation of wrong there must be an equal understanding of right. In the beaver's life we see many instances of the observing of their unwritten laws. The right of possession is seldom questioned, thieving is not allowed, or at least not indulged in. Community interests are understood, so that all members of a colony, whether comprising one family or many, will assist in work which is obviously for the benefit of all, such as building and repairing the dams, which are apparently common property, while in contrast to this they do not help in building each other's lodges. Each lodge belongs to those who expect to occupy it, and by them alone is it erected and repaired. In case of danger the one who first suspects it has

thought for the others and immediately warns
them by slapping the water. Foster parentage
is not uncommon among beaver ; where a mother
has been killed her young are taken care of by
others that have young themselves, an exhibition
of the noblest form of charity which entails a great
amount of labour and worry upon the foster
mothers and fathers. The more one sees of wild
animals the more one is forced, if not blinded by
prejudice and other equally blighting forms of
ignorance, to realise and admire the beauty of
their natures. And just as we are in danger, as
Darwin says, of underrating " the mental powers
of the higher animals," so are we too oft averse
to crediting them with a sufficiently well-developed
moral nature.

Taking all things into consideration the beaver
may be said to be one of the most peaceful of
animals, even cowardly according to some observers.
Yet this is scarcely a fair statement for any man to
make. Under ordinary conditions the beaver will
avoid any exhibition of pugnacity. Even when
caught in a trap they will watch the approach of
the trapper without signs of resentment or fear,
though they probably know that his coming means
their death. As he approaches they neither snarl
nor bite, but with a pathetic appeal in their mild
eyes simply put up their little hands above their
heads as though to ward off the fatal blow of the
axe or club. A more touching spectacle would be

hard to imagine and yet, see the same creature when danger threatens its young. See how careless it is of its own safety; thinking, just as many birds do, only to decoy the enemy away, it will approach to within a few feet of man and feign a crippled condition, falling down and showing every evidence of powerlessness. Almost will it allow itself to be caught if the danger to the young seems imminent, and so it will coax its enemy further and further, while the subject of all this solicitude watches a suitable opportunity, and vanishes the very moment it finds it is not observed. No sooner is it in safety than the parent regains her vigour and makes off with all possible speed. Evidently the beaver is not a coward, but a born believer in peace, a suitable emblem for all peace conferences, for it believes in industrious, not lazy, peacefulness, and is thoroughly against everything in the way of fights and conflicts. It asks only to be left alone when it will work unceasingly in the accomplishment of what the Designer of the world intended it should do.

CHAPTER III

RESULTS OF BEAVERS' WORK — IN WHAT WAY
MAN DERIVES BENEFIT FROM THE ENGINEER-
ING FEATS OF THE COUNTLESS GENERATIONS
OF BEAVERS—METHODS FOR THEIR PROTECTION

IN the foregoing chapters the actual work done
by the beaver and the immediate object of such
work as it affects the animals themselves has been
reviewed. We may now turn to the far-reaching
results of what is done, and has been done by them
during the past thousands of years, and the conclusion is forced upon us that the debt we owe to
the beaver is of such magnitude that it can never
be repaid. It is very doubtful indeed whether the
work of any animal has such far-reaching results.
Other creatures have been of greater value, either
as furnishing food, or clothing, or means of transportation, but by themselves, unaided by man, they
have done no work, they have accomplished little
or nothing which has been of any direct benefit to
man except in the way of killing our enemies, in
which work birds take the highest place, for without
their perpetual aid we should be overrun by insect
pests, and be unable to grow our food crops.
Slowly we are beginning to realise this and are

A dam when kept in repair retains the water of the pond almost to its extreme crown.

As a dam falls into decay the site becomes overgrown with alders and willows.

This dam, no longer kept in repair, will let the water escape, and before long will lose all semblance of its original form.

making a fight against the dastardly destruction of these innocents for purposes of personal adornments and other equally useless objects. But the beaver is almost without any champion. He even has enemies who demand that he shall be killed for the harm he does to their particular interests. They do not stop to consider how they benefit by the results of the little animals' work which far more than counter-balances any slight harm they do.

In this chapter I shall endeavour to show what the beavers' work means. The question of the value of the animals themselves as fur bearers, and the results to the country from their pursuit, will come in a later chapter. We have seen that through making dams the beaver floods tracts of land which vary in size from less than an acre up to hundreds of acres, perhaps we might even say thousands. So long as these ponds or lakes are inhabited by the animals the dams are kept in repair, but gradually, as the size of the colony increases, the supply of food trees becomes more and more remote and the place eventually is unsuited to their needs, so the beaver move away and seek new pastures. In the natural course of events the dam, no longer kept in repair, soon begins to break down. Willows and alders take root and open up seams through which the water escapes. Running water soon enlarges any holes in earth works, and so within a short time the dams no longer hold back the water, the pond gets lower and lower until finally it vanishes.

So much for the dam ; now let us watch the pond itself throughout its course of existence. It began as a stream whose banks were probably wooded. As the water rose and flooded the land the trees, which had not been cut for food by the beavers, becoming choked by water soon died, and as the pond grew with each year's additions to the dams, more and more trees were cut down for food and killed by water. What started as a pond of perhaps fifty feet wide and covering far less than an acre becomes a lake of fair size. Gradually the trees that have died fall and no trace of them is seen above water. Their roots may remain hidden in the ground to be dug up later as proof of the previous existence of the trees. Nothing remains to break the smooth surface of the lake except perhaps one or more beaver islands on which the lodges were built. After the place has been occupied by many generations of beaver it is abandoned owing to lack of food, or for the more dismal reason that the trapper had paid his visits of destruction to the peaceful colony, and the pond of maybe ten or a hundred years' growth slowly subsides. During all these years there has been a rich land-forming process going along in an automatic way. The growing vegetation, having been killed by the rising water, has decomposed. Wood and leaves, grasses and roots, and even stones have become a homo-

geneous mass of material which under certain
conditions makes soil. Year after year the trees on
the surrounding hills and valleys have shed their
myriad leaves, and these have been blown into the
lake, or carried to it by the rains and melting snows.
Débris of all sorts has been brought down to the
flooded areas where in the still waters it all settles
to the bottom so that gradually a deep vegetable
muck has formed over the land that once was
covered with trees and flowers and richly coloured
mosses. Most of this refuse of the woods is under
normal conditions carried down by the various
streams into the rivers and so out to the sea and
apparently man gets no benefit from it. But the
beaver lake has arrested this valuable material and
prevented it going to waste. Instead of being lost
it has been stored up, not in one pond, but in
hundreds of thousands, large and small. With the
desertion of a beaver pond the water, as already
stated, being no longer held in check by the well-
built dams, gradually finds its way out. The sub-
sidence may be slow or rapid, but the effect is the
same. The whole area of flooded land begins to
dry, and what was formerly a rough irregular
tract has become smooth and level. For some
time the water-soaked land is too heavy to allow of
a good growth of vegetation, but it is opened and
ploughed by the winter frosts, while the sun and the
rains prepare it for its great mission. Grasses take
possession and soon the lake becomes a meadow

luxuriant, smooth and beautiful, a visible result of the beavers' industry and the super-human direction of the power which controls all material things, and produces the greatest results from the smallest and most insignificant beginnings.   How many acres of the finest meadow land and richest valleys are the result of beavers' work no one dare say.   But throughout North America it is fairly safe to say that many hundreds of thousands, or even millions of acres, of the finest cultivated land owe their existence to the beaver.   Of course in most places all trace of the origin of these bottom lands is lost, but every once in a while a beaver-cut stump is discovered by those who have to dig down a few feet below the surface, and in some cases these evidences of beaver work have been found fully thirty or forty feet down, where for countless ages they have been preserved by the peat which has formed over them.   Agassiz, speaking of the age of beaver work, mentions the building of a mill dam which necessitated some excavating.   "This soil was found to be peat bog.   A trench was dug into the peat twelve feet wide, by twelve hundred feet long, and nine feet deep; all the way along this trench old stumps of trees were found at various depths, some still bearing marks of having been gnawed by beaver teeth."   By calculating the growth of the bog as about a foot a century there is fairly good evidence that the dam built by the beaver must have existed about one thousand years ago.

A beaver pond seen from an elevation. The lodges are seen on the extreme right.

A comparatively new beaver pond filled with trees which have been killed by the water. These will gradually disappear and leave the pond unobstructed.

When the dam begins to disintegrate the pond rapidly dwindles to an insignificant size.

Do the farmers realise what debt they owe to the beaver ? I fear not. Their one idea if a beaver is found anywhere within their property is to immediately kill it. For they regard its wretched skin, worth perhaps ten dollars at most, as being the only value of the beaver, and so the wretched beast is caught and its skin saved, while the brains which have accomplished so much are thrown to the dogs. Who is to blame for this ? Those who have the teaching of our children. If only the schools taught more about the usefulness of animals and birds, even from the selfish point of view of their results to men, and taught these things intelligently, much good would come. But a trip into any part of the country where the beaver still exists in its wild state will show how blind people are to their own interest in allowing these animals to be destroyed.

Before going further into this side of the question it might be as well to show some more ways in which the beaver is of almost unlimited benefit to mankind and the country in general. Water, as we well know, is the most essential of all things ; on its supply a country thrives or perishes. Millions of pounds are spent annually to protect and conserve the supply, so that towns and farms, and forests too, shall have all that is needed. With the opening up of country and the consequent destruction of forest land, the supply is inevitably bound to decrease, as the thousands of smaller streams are deprived of the shelter which prevents the rapid evaporation of the water ; the result is of course the lessening of the amount in the larger rivers.   At certain seasons the supply is too great, and floods do infinite damage. At other times there is a great shortage.   Man, in order to prevent this uneven supply, builds enormous dams which retain the water during the season of plenty, and deal it out as needed during the hot summer months.   But even with man's most carefully arranged plans and vast expenditure of money, we hear of periodic water famines, with the resulting hardships which have such far-reaching and disastrous results.   But what, may be asked, has this got to do with beaver ?   A glance at the work of those small animals will answer the question. Their dams, built most often near the head waters of streams, result in countless reservoirs, which keep the water in check and allow only the *steady* flow of a small amount, so that droughts in a beaver country are almost unknown, as there is always a sufficient supply kept in reserve.   In some few parts of the country stock owners have begun to realise this important fact with the highly satisfactory result that these men are protecting beaver, which they regard as of the utmost value, because they can actually *see* the benefits which result from the work of these insignificant engineers.   In the western States this exhibition of the importance of the beaver is most in evidence, and we may hope that other parts of the country will eventually, and before it is too late, follow in the footsteps of those men in South Dakota and other places who have set such good example.

Apart from the conserving of water, the dams play another and almost equally important part. Floods, as already stated, are a source of almost unlimited trouble to both the farmer, the lumberman, and the villages. In fact everyone may indirectly suffer from the effects of too much water. Bridges are destroyed, roads rendered impassable and endless confusion is the result. The following piece of news is more eloquent than any words of mine on the subject. It appeared in the *Gazette* (Montreal) in the issue of September 9th, 1913. Curiously enough, I was on my way to carry on my studies of beaver in Ontario when it happened to catch my eye.

Bursting of Beaver Dam.

CAUSE OF BIG SLIDES ON CANADIAN PACIFIC.

" Vancouver, B.C., September 8.—All trains held up on the main line of the Canadian Pacific by slides are now on their way east and west. The line was finally cleared at eleven o'clock this morning. Yesterday the population of Field, the town nearest the slide, which occurred between Pallises and Glenogle, 25 miles west of Field, was increased by the addition of 2,000 passengers who were held up by the delay.

"The slide, which was 300 feet wide and 30 feet deep, was caused by the bursting of an old beaver dam high up in the mountains. District Supt. MacKay, at Revelstoke, says that the dam burst under the pressure of heavy rain storms last week. The slide carried the track away completely and it went clear across the Kicking Horse River, damming that stream and endangering the track above the slide. The river was completely blocked up, and it was found necessary to blast a new channel for the stream to release the pent-up waters which threatened to cause a washout further east.

"The Canadian Pacific Railway had two steam shovels and a hundred men at work. Huge trees were brought down with the slide and boulders nearly as big as a box car made the job of clearing the track a difficult one. Some of the trees that came down bore the marks of the little animals' teeth, and the supports of the dam erected by the beavers were plainly marked as such by the bleaching of their upper ends and the lower points coated with mud and slime.

"Those of the delayed westbound passengers who arrived this morning expressed themselves as very well satisfied with the manner in which they were treated by the company.

"Fourteen trains, east and west-bound, were stalled by the slide. Some of the passengers were transferred across the wash slide over a narrow footbridge, and others who were bound east were routed

Eventually nothing of the pond remains, and the stream resumes its long-interrupted course.

What was originally forest land, then for many years a beaver pond or lake, becomes a rich meadow, which is ultimately devoted to the use of man.

down the Arrow Head Lakes and by way of the Crow's Nest Pass east again over the main line."

It is fairly safe to presume that the builders of the large dam had been killed some time ago, so that the structure, no longer in repair, broke under the pressure of the water. And yet the railway people are bitterly opposed to beavers being allowed to exist, because occasionally the animals dam the culverts, and so raise the water against the railroad embankments. No credit is given to them for the thousands of floods which they have prevented. The evil and not the good is noticed and the animals are condemned without a fair hearing. Their side of the case is too often entirely disregarded, and the sentence of death is pronounced to the misfortune of all concerned. I have frequently heard it argued by those interested in the lumber industries of Canada that the beaver should be killed off because they destroy so much timber. Even to the casual observer such an argument must appear little less than ridiculous. If the beaver is to be condemned on that score what might be said of the lumberman whose reckless waste of timber is apparent to all who visit the northern woods. But that is not a subject for this book. Our interest is in the beaver. Of course they cut down trees, cut them down in order that they may have food, just as the lumberman does that he and his family may live and earn a decent livelihood. The question is what sort of trees the beaver cut, and are they responsible for any real destruction ? I doubt it. To begin with, the principal trees cut for food purposes are birch, maple and poplars of several species which grow in low lands or in valleys, where their development is seldom great. Only on the higher ground, known as "hardwood ridges," do they attain a size which gives them a commercial value, so as a matter of fact few, if any, of the trees cut down by the beaver would ever be utilized by man. The greatest destruction is due to the killing of conifers by flooding their roots, and in this way we must acknowledge that a certain amount of damage may be charged against the beaver. But even so it is so slight that it is scarcely worth considering, except as an excuse for those who wish a pretext for voting against the preservation of the little animals, and whose actual reason is too often that they want the few dollars which the pelts might bring them.

Having barely suggested three of the most beneficial results of beaver work (I say barely suggested, for the subject might well be carried much further and many facts and figures given which would prove the points still more convincingly) we might now turn to the less important effects of the work. Everyone who has ever been much in the wilds knows the value of water-ways. In a canoe a man may travel with but little trouble, and may even allow himself many comforts that are debarred from the pack if weight has to be considered. Every portage, when canoeing, is an undesirable change from the quiet monotony of paddling, so the wise man chooses, so far as he is able, a route which will allow the canoe to remain in the water as much as possible. Such a man knows the value of going through beaver country. Streams which might otherwise be dry, especially during the summer months, can usually be counted on to have enough water to float a canoe if the beavers' dams are in repair, and so many a weary mile of portaging is avoided. Hundreds of miles have I travelled by canoe either alone or with some hardy woodsman, and hundreds of times I have blessed the little beaver for the streams he has kept filled. During such journeys, each time a dam is reached the canoe is hauled over it so that it shall do as little damage as possible, and by the paint marks on the sharp-pointed sticks I have known that many another man has had reason to bless the builders of those dams.

One other man who has reason to wish the preservation of the beavers is the fisherman, as the deep pools made along the waterways offer a cool retreat for the trout during the hot weather, and even though it may be said that the dams restrict the freedom of the fish in going up and down stream there are opportunities during the course of each year when the water overflows to such an extent that they can get past almost any dam. The fishermen, therefore, should use their influence in urging protection for the conservers of water.

Another and seldom considered result of beavers' work is the effect it has on the topography of a country. Fresh streams and rivers are made and old ones diverted to an extraordinary extent by the building of dams and consequent forming of ponds. Even new springs are brought to the surface by the pressure of the water in these ponds. Land-slides are prevented by reducing the force of streams, and in many ways quite unknown to us the con-tinued work of the beaver has had its varied effects on the land.

The whole question of preserving the beaver should receive most serious attention, for even apart from the sentimental side which deserves consideration, the practical value of the animals is undeniable. The idea of protecting the beaver is of long standing. As far back as 1634 in the Jesuit Relations, there are the following paragraphs :

" We (the Jesuits) shall be able to instruct them (the Indians) easily and Beaver will greatly multiply. These animals are more prolific than our sheep in France, the females bearing as many as five or six each year. But when the savages find a lodge of them they kill all, great and small, male and female. There is danger that they will finally exterminate the species in this region (Three Rivers) as has happened among the Hurons who have not a single beaver, going elsewhere to buy

An example of a diminishing lake and corresponding increase in the size of the "beaver meadow."

A beaver pond which may eventually become meadow land.

the skins they bring to the storehouse of these gentlemen." "Now if it will be so arranged that in the course of time each family of our Montaignais, if they become located, will take its own territory for hunting, without following in the tracks of its neighbours : besides we will counsel them not to kill any but the males "—(this is amusing advice as the two sexes cannot be told apart by their appearance)—" and of those only such as are large. If they act upon this advice they will have meat and skins in the greatest abundance." In another volume of the same work we find that Father Le Jeune (1636) offers a suggestion in the following words : " In time, parks can be made in which to keep Beaver ; these would be treasure-houses, besides furnishing us with meat at all times."

It is true that to-day the prospect for their welfare is better than it was some years ago when their extermination seemed to be imminent. Fourteen years ago I spent weeks travelling by canoe through what was formerly one of the best beaver countries in Canada, in search of material for some drawings on beaver and their work, and though I had with me an experienced Indian, I only found one colony, a small one, in a pond many miles north-west of Lake Temiscaming. All other ponds found on this trip were deserted, nothing but the decaying lodges and dams marked the places where the beavers had been. Trappers had relentlessly pursued them from pond to pond, and scarcely any remained, notwithstanding the fact that they were even then supposed to be protected by law. In a big wild country it is far easier to make than enforce laws, especially as the law prohibiting the killing of the beaver was obnoxious to so many whose living depended largely on the trapping or selling furs, for of all fur-bearers the most easily obtained are the beaver. The law was in fact almost a dead letter as very few were interested in its being observed. About that time in Canada certain men began to realise the value of proper game reserves, and be it said to their everlasting credit they succeeded in influencing the Government to carry out their ideas. In the United States, Colonel Roosevelt was one of those most active in the work of con-servation and in establishing reservations, and if he had done nothing else during his strenuous life he would be remembered by what he did in that direction. In Canada, several great "parks" or reserves were established, one particularly I know of which was designed for a "fish and game pre-serve, health resort and pleasure ground for the benefit, advantage and enjoyment of the people of Ontario, and for the protection of the fish, birds, game and fur-bearing animals therein," etc. Leaving aside all other animals and birds, we will see how it affected the beaver. The tract chosen was admirably adapted to their needs, and they soon found themselves, as they thought, safe from the continual dread of the steel trap, so that new colonies established themselves and increased most wonderfully. But the wretched beasts were lulled into a false security, and what followed for obvious reasons cannot be recounted here. Sufficient is it to say that great numbers of beavers were killed *by authority*, the number caught and killed in a single year I dare not mention, but under the clause which reads: " Upon the report of the Minister that any species of fur-bearing or game animal or bird has increased to such an extent that its numbers may be lessened without detriment to the Park, or the purposes for which the Park was established, the Lieutenant-Governor in Council may authorise the taking or killing of such animals or birds not exceeding the number specified in Order in Council under the direction and supervision of the Superintendent of the Park," and further, in speaking of furs, skins, etc., " May be sold by the Minister and the proceeds of the sales shall be applied toward defraying the expenses of the Park." The unfortunate and, I venture to add, injudicious taking of beaver has continued. The results are unsatisfactory from two points of view. First, that the beaver has been captured in *the most accessible parts of the park*, so that one of the objects of the reserve is defeated. The underlying idea was that in protecting the wild animals, and so bringing them to a condition of comparative tameness, the people who came to this "fish and game preserve, health resort and pleasure ground" should have an opportunity of seeing the wild animals, the most interesting of all being the beaver, whose works are a positive education for young and old. But these people, of whom I have met many, are filled with disappointment and disgust when they are shown abandoned dams and lodges close to the resorts (within a few hundred yards of hotels and camps) and are told that the builders themselves have been trapped and either killed or sent away to zoological gardens or other parts. Such treatment is scarcely fair to the people and cannot be considered wise. The country is certainly rich enough to support the parks without the necessity of getting money from the sale of the animals which the people would far rather see alive and in their natural conditions than in "returns for sale of skins." But the second objection is even more far-reaching though more subtle, because people do not generally grasp its significance. The trapper is told that the beaver are absolutely protected by law and that to kill one involves the offender in serious trouble, such as imprisonment, fine and confiscation of his traps. In other words, by strict Government orders beaver *may not be killed.* These trappers are usually men of fair-play who understand rude justice better than obscure reasonings. They believe that what is food for the goose is food for the gander, and that if they, who trap only as a means of livelihood may not kill beaver neither must anyone else, except possibly as specimens for museums or such special purpose, but that the Government should indulge in beaver killing for commercial reasons is past their understanding. To fully appreciate what I am speaking of it might be well to explain the situation a little more clearly. The land which has been set apart as a game reserve and park was formerly occupied by trappers who made their living out of the wild lands. According to their unwritten law, a man on establishing a claim has a right to a certain tract of country for trapping purposes. These rights are regarded as almost sacred, and the man who poaches on another's boundary is held to be little better than a thief. These rights go from father to son, with the understanding, I believe, that if the land is not trapped for a specified number of years, the privilege is forfeited. In order to get possession of a desirable tract, men will go great distances and endure untold hardships, with the understanding that once they have succeeded in finding what they want it is to be theirs, unless sold by the Government. It will be seen by this that the best trappers who for years had set their line of traps through the land which is now a park felt their expulsion very severely. To make amends to them a few were taken on as rangers or wardens. The men, though feeling themselves in hard luck, realised at heart that it

was after all for a good purpose, for well enough
they knew that unless the beaver was protected
it would be but a few years before they would be
a thing of the past, gone to join the dodo and
others that used to be.   So they took their
medicine like men, but when they saw that the
park was being used for trapping purposes, and
that the skins were being sold by the Government,
their spirits rose in rebellion.   More especially
when they themselves as employees of the park
had to take part in trapping the animals.   They
were for the most part quite willing to forego
their share of beavers' skins *if* the beaver was
to be really protected, but they do not see the
fairness of the present situation, and the result is
that men who otherwise would have honestly
observed laws which were for the welfare of the
greater number are now in many instances doing
their best to get a share of the spoils.   They do
not see that it is any longer a question of honour,
for if beaver *may* be killed, why should not they
as well as anyone else, reap the benefit ?   Laws
relating to wild animals in a great country which
has so small a population and so much wild land
can only be of real value if they are in accordance
with popular opinion, but just as soon as the public
considers a law unfair the difficulties of enforcing
that law become practically insurmountable.   What
I have written is not a matter of theory, but is the
result of observation and conversation with the

A fresh beaver-cut stump, showing the keen cutting through the hard birch.

Lodge built by beaver in the Washington Zoo.

Dam built by beaver in the Washington Zoo.

men interested in the question. There is absolutely no desire to tread on anybody's toes, but rather to call attention to conditions which might so easily be remedied, for my interest is simply with the beaver, and with protection of wild life in general.

I know it has been asserted that beaver were too abundant in a certain park, but whether the assertion was justified by facts I have serious doubts. At any rate, before radical measures were adopted, it would have been advisable to have had the expert opinion of an entirely disinterested person, or, better still, of many persons, and if their findings resulted in a disagreement then the beaver should have had the benefit of the doubt.

In Newfoundland the question of beaver protection needs most serious consideration and a definite policy lined out for future plans. Eleven years ago I first visited that country, and each succeeding year until 1912, when I was last there. During that period of ten years ample opportunities were afforded me of observing the beaver and the extraordinary results of what protection can do. During the first four visits to the island *I never saw but one beaver colony*, and that a very small one in a remote and inaccessible part of the country. In 1912 I counted no less than twenty-seven occupied lodges within a short day of walking and canoeing. What has happened in that one district is simply an indication of what might be expected elsewhere, and goes to show how rapidly the whole

country might be re-colonised by the interesting
animals.   Their abundance would be a great source
of pleasure to all who visit the delightful island,
and would add one more to the list of attractions
which it has to offer.   The one condition which
has retarded the increase of the beaver is that the
law for their protection has been so often changed.
The harm done is that each time the close season
was drawing to an end, beavers were surreptitiously
killed in anticipation of the time when the skins
might legally be offered for sale.   Then almost at
the last moment the close season would be extended
for another few years, very much to the disgust of
those who were storing skins at considerable risk,
for, justly enough, their discovery would mean a
heavy fine.   It can scarcely be doubted that fair
numbers of beaver were killed by those who wanted
to be ahead of their neighbours, for competition
must have been keen.

An animal which is as easily trapped or in other
ways killed, as the beaver, requires the most careful
protection, and laws should be considered with the
most thorough understanding of the conditions
governing their life and the trappers' powers.   Had
the close season (in Newfoundland) terminated two
years ago, the entire good gained by the preceding
years would have been lost.   For the trapper,
having learned by experience that laws can be made
and suddenly changed for the protection of the
beaver, would have made the most of the oppor-

tunity and practically every colony would have been
sacked within a very few months, and small indeed
would have been the number of survivors. How
to devise a sound scheme which would be fair on both
trapper and beaver is no easy task. But the Government has been so careful and far-sighted in its game
laws, having set a standard which might well be
considered by other countries, that I offer these
suggestions with due humility in the hope that
they may do some good. To open up a definite
tract of country for a certain period has the
disadvantage that it would mean the killing off of
every beaver in that tract, and would entail a great
deal of expense to the Government in the way of
patrols in order to prevent poaching in the closed
territory. Probably the soundest scheme would
be to licence every trapper, and furnish him with a
limited number of labels, one to be attached to
every beaver skin before allowing it to be sold.
This would serve the double purpose of limiting the
number of beaver killed, and keeping track of the
total amount with the least expense. Of course it
would be necessary to make the selling of any un-
labelled skins absolutely illegal, with punishment
severe enough to make it effective. Imprisonment
alone could do that, as the penalty would be most
likely to fall on those to whom the very name of
prison is most appalling. The number of labels
issued should be strictly limited with due reference
to the number of beaver. No beaver should be

taken until they are thoroughly established and really abundant, neither should they ever be molested in the reserves under any conditions, in order that people might have the opportunity of seeing them living peacefully and without suspicion. Fortunately they are amenable to protection and they adapt themselves readily to new conditions. In zoological gardens and private parks they do remarkably well, even though they can never be said to be show animals in any sense of the word when in captivity, owing to their crepuscular and nocturnal habits.

The following account of an experience I had with beaver in the Washington Zoological Gardens may be of interest, for even though it was published elsewhere many years ago it still shows something of the animal in captivity.

THE OUTCAST *

A TRUE STORY OF A CAPTIVE BEAVER

It is difficult to imagine a more pathetic sight than that of the poor old beaver solitary and so entirely alone, within sight of his comrades yet not among them, unable to join in their games and their work, living his lonely life like a hermit; within sight of his fellow men, but separated by a barrier as strange as it was secure. After I had waited for many hours watching quietly in the

* First published in *Everybody's Magazine.*

The outcast.

A rough example of beaver lodge in which very little sod or mud has as yet been used.

Type of lodge built on an island.

small enclosure above the large beaver pond in the Washington Zoo, there was a movement in front of the large hollow opening out on the water, and a head peeped out to see that all was safe for the owner's regular evening exercise. The sun had long since disappeared behind the hill and everything had the quiet hush of evening. The deep roaring of the lions and tigers and the more distant barking of the seals alone disturbed this silence, when the beaver, fancying himself alone, plunged noiselessly into the water, diving beneath the log that lay partly submerged but a few feet from the narrow entrance and reappeared in the middle of the small pond. Almost like a short piece of drift wood he lay with his tiny dark eyes gazing intently at me where I stood in the shadow of a small tree. Observing no movement and not being of a suspicious nature he soon swam to shore and immediately walked, moving for all the world like a large smoothly coated Canadian porcupine, straight to the corner of the fence that divided him from his relatives. Once there he stood on his hind legs and tail, and with front feet resting on the horizontal bar, he gazed, with a longing wistful look shown by his entire attitude, at the lodge in which the other beavers lived. Never surely was loneliness shown more eloquently than by this soft furred animal as he stood there, the very picture of solitude in the midst of so many, as a stranger in a city where the fences of convention, bars as rigid as those which surrounded this beaver, keep him from personal intercourse with his fellow men.   For ten minutes he remained thus, motionless except when, as though no longer able to contain his misery, he would bite the hard, cold bars of iron, as he had bitten them every evening for three, long, weary months.   Did he imagine that perhaps some day he would find the bars had softened and would yield to his chisel-edged teeth, teeth that, were the animal in his native land, would work their way through anything save the stones or the cruel metal of the merciless steel traps?   These alone would defy them.

Wishing to examine more closely the interesting animal I approached quietly, hoping not to disturb him, but he felt uncertain of my intentions, and before I had lessened the distance between us by more than a few steps, he dropped on all fours, and after regarding me curiously for a minute or two turned and made for the water.   Once there he felt more secure, for at the slightest sign of danger he would, as he had done many times in his far-off Canadian wilds, dive in and loudly slap the water with his tail to warn his friends and then instantly disappear from view beneath the water and make straight for his burrow.   His curiosity, however, soon got the better of his natural timidity, and out he came with the usual quiet splash and dive.   This time I stood near his regular landing place, which was as clearly marked as an otter's slide, and wondered whether he would venture near. Slowly he swam towards me, stopping repeatedly to investigate. What it was that gave him confidence I could not tell, but suddenly he apparently made up his mind that there was no occasion for fear and he moved quickly, landing within three feet of where I stood. Once on shore he again doubted the wisdom of his course and hesitated, not quite liking to pass so near a human being ; sitting half way up on his hind legs and tail with his small fore paws held close beneath his chin he carefully watched me, his nose moving slowly as though trying to scent an enemy. A few minutes sufficed for this, and then we had established a degree of mutual confidence at once satisfactory and useful, for I hoped on the following day to take a few photos of my new friend, and it is highly desirable that we should be on a footing of trust with our model. It was rapidly becoming dark, too dark, indeed, for me to distinguish much more than the general form of the beaver. So I left him to his thoughts, intending to visit him again the following afternoon.

That the reader may understand something of the position of this poor old hermit a few words of explanation are needed. When the beavers were first brought to the Zoo they were given for their new home a small enclosure of perhaps two acres. Through this ran a very small stream, the banks of which were fairly well wooded. It was but a short time before the industrious animals commenced work; the stream was so small that they were unable even to swim in it, so a dam was planned and rapidly constructed. Trees were felled, some of which were nearly eighteen inches in diameter; from these the branches were cut, then divided into convenient lengths and used in the dam building; the bottom of the stream was dredged and the mud and roots used to finish off the structure and make it watertight. The number of trees decreased so rapidly through the industry of those four-footed engineers that it became necessary to protect those that still remained unharmed with heavy wire netting. This at first was fastened to the tree in direct contact, but it was soon discovered that the beavers could cut the tree between the meshes. To prevent this an iron rail, to which the wire was attached, was placed at a little distance from the tree. The dam was by this time fairly large, but not as large as was needed. More material was needed, so a great quantity of cut wood was thrown into the enclosure and was immediately utilised by the beavers; in a short time the level of the water was raised many feet with the result that a pond of considerable dimensions was formed. Three other dams were also built down stream from the main structure, about fifty feet apart. It was late summer by the time this work was accomplished, and a house had to be built with as little delay as possible, for with

Repairing a broken dam. The beaver is forcing a heavy piece of water-soaked wood into the breach ; in so doing he touched the thread which was connected with the electric trigger of the flashlight.

A subsidiary or secondary dam built to support the main structure, which may be seen on the middle and right side of the upper part of the picture.

the arrival of cold weather all building operation must cease as the mud freezes and of course becomes too hard to work. The house or lodge, as it is more properly named, is outwardly a great mass of loose sticks, some of which might from their size be called logs, filled in with earth and roots and covered over with mud. In the centre very little mud is used, for there is a sort of irregular chimney, which serves as a ventilator. Inside the house all is darkness or very nearly so. The walls are rough, but the floor, which is raised a few inches above the water, is firm and smooth, made of fine twigs beaten into the earth. The entrances, for there are usually two or more, are several feet beneath the water. What impressed me on seeing the lodge and dams built by the beavers in the Washington Zoo was the fact that in no way did they differ from those in the most remote part of Canada.

When spring came it was found that the beavers had increased in numbers, very much to the delight of all concerned, but the following year, when they were all full grown, the rules and regulations of beaverdom were put in force. They decided that there was one too many, and according to their laws he must either betake himself to some other locality or submit to an untimely death. Now, the victim chosen—whether by ballot or by whatever means who can say ?—was our old friend, and as it was impossible for him to leave the colony of his own accord, death would have been his lot had not the keeper come to the rescue and given him a cage where he might live until a better place could be provided. It was two or three months before he was turned into the enclosure in which I found him. This bordered on his old home and was separated only by an iron fence. Being a solitary bachelor he has not as yet set up housekeeping ; perhaps he thinks it scarcely worth while building a house until he has a mate. As it is he has made a burrow in the bank with the entrance at the level of the water. In this he spends his days, seldom coming out at all before sunset, frequently much later. When out he spends much of his time watching his old companions, while they in turn seem to take but little notice of him. So much for the reason of his being alone.

On the occasion of my second visit to this solitary beaver I brought my camera, with the fond hope of being able to secure a few photographs, even though the light might not be suitable for such work. It was nearly five o'clock before he made his appearance, and then, as on the day previous, after emerging from his burrow, he lay quietly on the water taking in the situation before daring to come ashore. I had placed the camera so that if he went to his usual corner it would not be necessary to move it. After satisfying himself that all was well he landed and walking past the camera took up his position at the fence corner.

Standing erect as on the previous day he gazed
intently at the home of his old friends. They had
not yet made their appearance, but from their lodge
came the sound of muffled voices, for they were
holding an animated conversation in beaver lan-
guage, which sounds like a strange subdued mixture
of children's voices and very young pigs squealing,
varied now and then by a puppy's cry. Whether
or not our beaver understood the drift of their dis-
cussion would be difficult to say, but certain it is
that he seemed to be very much interested by it
all. While he stood there almost as motionless as a
statue, I made several exposures, bringing the camera
nearer and nearer each time; when within almost
five feet he turned round to examine the strange
one-eyed monster that was approaching so quietly.
It evidently puzzled him without frightening him.
After a few moments his curiosity got the upper
hand and he came straight for it, slowly of course,
and hesitating slightly at each step. As he came
nearer I retreated that I might the better see what
he would do. To begin with each leg of the tripod
was scrutinised most carefully; these he evidently
concluded were harmless, so resting his hands on
one of the legs he reached up and took a good look
at the camera itself. His nose must have discovered
some new odour, for he sniffed first on one side
then on the other for many minutes; suddenly his
attention was attracted by the rubber ball belong-
ing to the shutter. This was moving at the end

of the tube, and he thought that perhaps it was something new in the way of food. In another moment the bulb would have been rendered useless, for his sharp teeth would have instantly punctured it. At this critical moment I had to interfere, very much to his disgust, as the poor old chap evidently thought he had been robbed of a delicious morsel, and I regretted not having brought a carrot or sweet potato for him. Wishing to make friends with this strange animal, I sat down near the camera. Immediately he came near, so near that I could put my hand on his soft, furry back, wondering at the time what would happen if he should take it into his head to use his teeth. For with their extraordinary strength and sharpness the amputation of a finger or two would have been the work of an instant ; however, he was a very well meaning old fellow and contented himself with walking slowly round me, stopping occasionally to sit on his hind legs and take a general survey of the curious being who went about with the three-legged thing—the camera. Satisfied that he might safely leave me for a short while he went to his corner, and after looking for a few minutes at his neighbours who were swimming about in their pond he went down his path to the water's edge, and in his own peculiar, noiseless way, plunged in for a swim. He soon discovered a stick upon which some bark still remained. This he brought ashore and holding it with his front paws, or hands as they might well be called, proceeded to make a meal therefrom. It required but a few minutes to strip the stick of its bark, after which it served no further use and was left in the water while the animal swam around making a tour of investigation, which resulted in his not finding anything more suited to his taste. So coming ashore near where I stood, he commenced his evening toilet, which was interesting to watch. To begin with, instead of sitting with his large flat-ribbed tail protruding behind him he tucked it forward between his hind legs and sat upon it. Then with his hands he carefully combed his long fur, using both hands at the same time. There were, however, many places that he could not reach in this way, for his arms are very short. So with one hind foot at a time he combed these otherwise inaccessible parts ; the entire operation was performed with the utmost deliberation and care, and occupied nearly twenty minutes, so that by the time it was completed the daylight had almost vanished. My presence did not appear to disturb him in the very least, though I sat quite close that I might the better note his various attitudes, for it is not often one has an opportunity of watching a beaver at such close range. Suddenly the night watchman, whose duty it is to feed the nocturnal animals, arrived with a basket of stale bread and vegetables. These he threw into the enclosure, the vegetables on the bank and the bread into the pond. Mr. Beaver well understood the meaning of those splashes, for he instantly made for the water, utterly regardless of his newly dried jacket about which he had taken so much trouble, and seizing one of the loaves of bread in his hands swam to a shallow part of the pond to eat it. He held the bread in his hands, much after the manner in which a squirrel holds a nut, but the bread being wet began to fall apart so he made a bowl of his hands and lapped the soft bread out of it; in this way not a particle was lost. Piece after piece of bread was eaten, after which he came ashore and made short work of the carrots and potatoes. It was quite dark by this time, and as it was impossible to see anything more I was forced to leave him, with the hope that in the near future I might continue the acquaintance so pleasantly begun. When that day comes let us hope he will no longer be solitary but will have taken to himself a mate whose disposition will be as good as his own.

From what has been said in the preceding pages, it will be seen that the beaver is a gentle creature, free from desire to harm anybody. As pets they become extremely affectionate and dependent on their masters. Mills* describes an interesting experience with a pet beaver to which he became deeply attached. "Atop the pack on the horse's back he travelled,—a ride which he evidently

* "In Beaver World."

enjoyed. He was never in a hurry to be taken off, and at moving time he was always waiting eagerly to be lifted on. As soon as he noticed me arranging the pack, he came close, and before I was quite ready for him he rose up, extending his hands in rapid succession beggingly, and with a whining sort of muttering pleaded to be lifted at once to his seat on the pack." There are many instances of Indians having tame beavers, some of which grew up in the family having been taken as kittens and nursed by the squaws. From this and all other accounts the beaver is shown to be a delightful pet, cleanly in habit, good-tempered, quiet and gentle. The only objection to them is their predilection for mistaking chair and table legs for growing trees and cutting them down. The fact that they cut down trees is rather a serious argument against having them at large in private parks. The only way to keep them and not suffer from their peculiar habits is to set aside a portion of a stream for their use, and have a vigorous growth of aspens or some equally quick-growing tree partitioned off into small lots. A low iron fence is sufficient to keep the beaver out and they could be allowed access to one part until they had fairly well cleared it of timber. A certain number of trees could always be safeguarded by means of wire netting. The animals, having to do the work of cutting, would keep in good condition, far healthier and more vigorous than if fed with cut up food. In order that the supply of growing trees be not too rapidly depleted, some scraps of brush or poles could be given occasionally. Sir Edmund Loder has a very ingenious scheme for feeding the small colony of beaver that he keeps in his fascinating place in Sussex. A small hole filled with several large stones serves as a holder for trees or poles or even stout branches, so that the beaver, in order to obtain the bark, must cut it down just as they would if it were a growing tree. Unfortunately most of this colony was carried away by a great flood, the animals being eventually killed in the sea by fishermen who were much puzzled by seeing such unusual creatures swimming about in the harbour. All large trees in a beaver enclosure must be very carefully protected, for no matter how large they may be, the beaver will girdle them and eat the bark. Most of the work done by the animals in their wild state will be almost equally well done in captivity, so that a small beaver colony is always an object of intense interest and may be maintained at comparatively small cost in money and labour.

It is to be hoped that as people realise more fully the interest and value of these animals they will take steps for their protection in all countries suited to their needs. It would indeed be a shame to see such creatures exterminated. There would be nothing to take their place, and I find wherever I go, and whatever class and age of people I am

A fine example of a woodland dam, 365 feet in length, of which about 70 feet was over 7 feet high.

In spite of the timidity of beaver they sometimes select curiously public places for their scene of operations. The dam shown in this picture is alongside a railroad embankment over which trains passed at frequent intervals.

Beavers' attempt to improve on man's work. The log dam was built by lumber men; the beaver did not approve, so they placed a small dam (shown near the rocks to the right of the centre), which held back the water to their complete satisfaction.

with, the subject of beaver and their work is always of interest, far more so than any other animal. For whether a person knows anything of animals or not, the extraordinary engineering feats of the beaver, their home life and habits, compel attention. It is a pity that there is not a broader knowledge on the subject, so that those who are in a way making their living from the results of the little animals' work should realise to whom they owe the debt.

When the first settlers came over to North America, they found a wilderness where they wanted to start their new homes. They most often selected what they considered the natural meadows for their homesteads. These broad valleys in which they found rich luxuriant grasses waving in the summer breezes appealed to them. In such places their cattle would feed in comfort and abundance. Hay too could be gathered to fill their rude barns, that their stock might be well fed during the long bitter winters. The meadows always contained a stream where the animals could be watered without trouble. In fact the pioneers found farms almost ready made, awaiting only the plough to turn the rich soil into the finest crop-producing land. And all without the tedious labour of clearing, and only those who have attempted such work can realise the amount of labour involved in clearing thickly timbered land. But a small part of the work can be done during

the slack winter season, during which time trees
are cut, but the hard stumps are frozen into the
ground, and not until the soft rains have thawed
the earth can they be removed. Rotting them out
is a slow process involving many years during
which cultivation of the stump-strewn land is
difficult and unsatisfactory. Blasting them out is
far too expensive for the poor settler, so that every
acre of ready cleared land means a tremendous saving
of labour; and what is even more important, the
forest land, though it may be fairly rich, does not
compare in fertility with that of the meadows, and
is of course usually so rough that cultivating is far
more difficult. But the farmer who thus reaped
the benefit of countless ages of beavers' work
had no thought for the little fellows. On every
possible occasion he trapped them, though perhaps
the very ones he killed were the direct descendants
of those that had originally built the dams which
had made the meadows for him and his family.
His house might even be built on the site of the
original lodges, and years later a village or a town
be built around the same place. Factory whistles
might scream to thousands of busy men and
women, calling them to begin or finish their day's
labour where formerly the evening call of the owl
had summoned forth the beaver to their night's
work. The saw mill on the old beaver pond might
screech as its many-toothed, buzzing saws tear
through the heart of the stoutest trees, in the very

Working on the lodge and carrying branches to the winter store, which is placed in the water and quite near the house. (*Painting.*)

The winter life of the beaver. As the pond and house are frozen and covered with snow, the animals obtain their food from the store which they collected and placed under water before the beginning of winter. (*Painting.*)

place where years ago the trees had been cut by the keen-edged teeth of the beaver. Ship canals might be built where the furry little engineers had built their canals. Great stone dams form reservoirs where the primitive earth and log dams had once held water for the beaver. We are a busy people and we can give but little heed to sentiment, but surely there is time in our lives to think of preserving and protecting the beaver. Let us hope that the generations who follow us will be able to thank us, their forefathers, for having defended the beaver when they look on these small creatures continuing the work their Creator intended they should do. We owe that much to our descendants, and we owe still more to the beaver.

CHAPTER IV

BEAVER AND CANADIAN HISTORY—SHOWING SOME-
THING OF THE PART PLAYED BY THEM IN THE
DEVELOPMENT OF THE COUNTRY

In reading the earlier history of Canada, we find
that from the very beginning, its development was
inextricably interwoven with the life or, I should
say, the death of the beaver. It lived on the
beaver. It was opened up by the beaver, wars
were waged through the competition for the skins
of the little animals, the skins were the currency of
the country, the clothing to some extent, and
frequently did the earlier inhabitants depend on its
meat for their food. In no country has an animal
played such a conspicuous part.

Going back to the first settlement of Canada, we
find that the beaver held an important place in the
life of the Indians. Their legends are full of
allusions to the animals, and some tribes believed
that the world was originally made by beaver, not
the same kind that we have now, but by gigantic
ones who were possessed of superhuman power.
Some legends state that the beaver is a reincarna-
tion of man, put back on earth to work for past
offences, and early drawings show the beaver with

men's faces. Some of the Indians themselves claim descent from beaver, and there are many stories of intermarriage between beavers and Indian women, and of the women bearing beaver children. One of the most famous of the Indian ritualistic medicine bundles was known as the " beaver-bundle." The owners of these curious assortments of objects were considered to have special powers, and were the weather men and almanac keepers. The origin of the bundles varies greatly according to the different tribes. One version only will be sufficient to give an idea of the legend, and is taken from Wissler and Duvall's *Blackfoot Mythology*.*

BLOOD VERSION.

" You say you have heard the story of Scabby-Round-Robe; but he did not first start the beaver-medicine, because it is said in the story that there was such a medicine before his time. The story I now tell you is about the origin of beaver-medicine.

" Once there was a man and his wife camping alone on the shore of a small lake. This man was a great hunter, and had in his lodge skins of almost every kind of bird and animal. Among them was the skin of a white buffalo. As he was always hunting, his wife was often left alone. One day a beaver came out of the water and made love to her.

* Published by the American Museum of Natural History in the series of Anthropological Papers. 1908.

This went on for some time, until finally she went away with the beaver to his home in the water. Now when the man came home, he looked all about for his wife, but could not find her anywhere. As he was walking along the shore of the lake, he saw her trail going down into the water. Now he knew what had happened. He did not break camp, but continued his hunting. After four days, the woman came up out of the water and returned to her lodge. She was already heavy with child. When her husband returned that evening, he found her in her usual place, and she told him all that had occurred.

" In the course of time the woman gave birth to a beaver. To keep it from dying she put it in a bowl of water, which she kept at the head of her bed. In the evening her husband came in as usual, and after a while, hearing something splashing in water, he said, ' What is that ? ' Then the woman explained to him that she had given birth to a beaver. She brought him the bowl. He took out the little beaver, looked at it, and put it back. He said nothing. As time went on he became very fond of the young beaver and played with him every evening.

" Now the beaver down in the water knew everything that was going on in the lodge. He knew that the man was kind to the young beaver, and so was not angry with him. He took pity on the man. Then the father of the young beaver resolved to give the man some of his medicine-songs in exchange for the skins of birds and animals the man had in his lodge. So one day, when the woman went down to the lake for water, the beaver came out and instructed her to request of her husband that whatever he [the beaver] should ask in his songs, that should be done. He also stated the time at which he would come to the lodge to be received by her husband.

" At the appointed time the beaver came out of the lake and appeared before the lodge, but, before he entered, requested that the lodge be purified [a smudge]. Then he entered. They smoked. After a while the beaver began to sing a song, in which he asked for the skin of a certain bird. When he had finished, the man arose and gave the bird-skin to him. Then the beaver gave another song, in which he asked for the skin of another bird, which was given him. Thus he went on until he secured all the skins in the man's lodge. In this way the man learned all the songs that belonged to the beaver-medicine and also the skins of the animals to which the songs belonged.

" After this the man got together all the different kinds of bird and animal skins taken by the beaver, made them up into a bundle, and kept the beaver-medicine."

Beaver robes were supposed to have certain virtues and were used in many ceremonies, especially

those in any way connected with death. Father
Paul Le Jeune states that they were used " for
what winding-sheets and shrouds are in France."
And in giving accounts of funeral rites he says :
" When the friends have gazed upon the bodies to
their satisfaction they cover them up with handsome
beaver robes, quite new." And again : " These
bones are enclosed in caskets of bark covered with
new beaver skins." When the Iroquois, Onagan,
delivered two captives over to Father Ragueneau,
he said, lifting up a beaver robe, " Behold the
standard that you shall plant upon your fort, when
you shall see our canoes appear upon this great
river ; and, when we see this signal of your friendship we shall land with confidence at your ports."
As presents, nothing approached in value the beaver
robe, not only on account of its actual worth, but
it seemed to be a sort of emblem. The Jesuit
priests, whose work in Canada during its early days
was so very remarkable, realised thoroughly the
sentimental value, both of these robes and the
single skins. These were apparently always accept-
able presents which carried with them some subtle
meaning. When disturbances occurred they gave
them as a seal of friendship. On one occasion when
there had been trouble with the Iroquois we find
that " in order to wipe out the blood, and implant
joy in every breast, leaving no trace of sadness anywhere, the Father presented four beaver skins to
the four Iroquois nations. One for each." The

intrinsic value of these skins was practically nothing, yet the giving of them meant a great deal. On another occasion, Father Ragueneau, in order to establish peace between two tribes made a gift of eight beavers to the Oneiotchronons at Three Rivers, " to exhort them to go to the chase without fear, and if they should meet the Algonquins

The beaver and peculiar ideas of lodges.
(From an old print, 1755.)

they shall prepare a kettle, and give one another meat."

In connection with the building of churches the beaver played an important part, and many edifices owe their existence to contributions of skins. " In the year 1645 Monsieur de Montmagny, the Governor, and the inhabitants gave twelve hundred and fifty beaver skins brought by the soldiers, who came from the Huron country, to have a church built at Kebec in honour of Our Lady of Peace."

The value of these skins was about 8,000 livres,
and the size of the church (which was probably the
original Parish Church of Quebec) was 30 by 100
feet. The churches were furnished indirectly by
the beaver, for we find that "in the year 1642
Monsieur de l'Isle, lieutenant of Monsieur the
Governor, gave a robe of beaver skins with which
were purchased the two pieces of carpet that lie
around the altar." From the same source (The
Jesuit Relations in Canada) there is given a pathetic
account of the early Christianity (1659) of the
Indians in which the beaver robes are mentioned.
" A good Christian Algonkin (also in other places
spelled Algonquin) woman named Cecile Koue-
koueaté, falling sick in the midst of the woods and
seeing herself in extremity without being able to
confess, she believed that she might make up for
this in some fashion with a present of beaver skins
which she bequeathed to the Church at Three
Rivers," sending this by her kinsmen who came
after her death to the priest. They spoke thus :
" Black Gown (as they called the priests), listen to
the voice of the dead and not to that of the living.
It is not we who speak to thee ; it is a departed
woman who before dying enclosed her voice in this
package. She charged it to declare to thee all her
sins, as she herself could not do by word of mouth.
Your handwriting enables you to speak to the
absent ; she intends to do so by these beaver skins
what you do with your papers," etc. A few years

Canal made by beaver in order to enable them to transport their wood cuttings from the source of supply to the pond in which the winter food supply is stored. (*Painting.*)

Rolling a log down their roadway to the pond, when it will be floated to the winter store. *(Painting.)*

later, there is another account of a poor woman
eighty years of age whose son had been slain,
sending in her little offering of " six beaver skins
in order to have prayers offered to God for his
soul."

It appears that the beaver skins caused serious
difficulties to the priests, who were practically
forced to use them as money and in many other
ways. Apparently private persons were unable to
send the skins to France, in fact they could not
dispose of them for shipment except through the
French company, which had such unlimited powers
and which presumably did not pay anything like
the price offered in Europe, so that the Jesuits
were forced to lose heavily in the transaction.
Father Le Jeune writes very strongly on this
question, and I quote rather fully from him as his
account has a direct bearing on the beaver and the
way in which the use and sale of the skins crept in
to all the dealings between France and Canada.
He begins with the statement, " The 7th general
congregation of our Society which absolutely for-
bids all kinds of commerce and business under any
pretext whatever," and further on, " Some of our
Fathers send me word that we must not even look
at from the corners of our eyes, or touch with ends
of our fingers, the skins of any of these animals
which are of great value here ; what can be the
cause of this advice ? " He then relates how they
have been slandered in France and says, " Peltry is

not only the best thing and the easiest to make use of in this country, but it is also the coin of greatest value.   And the best of it is that after it has been used as a covering * it is found to be ready-made gold and silver.   You know in France how much consideration is given to the style of a gown. Here all there is to do is to cut it out of a beaver skin and the savage woman straightway sews it to her little child with a moose tendon, with admirable promptness.   Who ever wishes to pay in this coin for the goods he buys here saves thereby the twenty-five per cent. that the market price gives them over that in France for the risk they run upon the sea—and certainly it seems that commutative justice allows that, if what comes to us from France is dearer for having floated over the sea, what we have here is worth something for having been chased in the woods and over the snow, and for being the wealth of the Country, especially as those who are paid with this coin always find therein their reckoning and something more." Twenty years later (1656-7) we find the situation has scarcely changed, as shown by the following extract from the Jesuit Relations : "That great council was held on the 24th of the month of July when all the Nation placed in the hands of Achiendasé (who is our Father Superior) the settlement of the difficulty between the Sonnon-

* The value of the skins for hatters' purposes is increased by their having been used.

toueronnons and the Annieronnons, which was soon ended. They then, with manifestations of extraordinary good will, agreed that we should establish ourselves and reside in their country. Finally each one deposited his presents in the war kettle. We had so well displayed, arranged and disposed our presents, that they made a wonderful show. It will not be out of place to observe in passing that these presents consist entirely of porcelain collars, beads, arquebuses, powder and lead, coats, hatchets, kettles, and other similar articles. These are purchased from the Merchants with beaver skins, which are the money that they demand in payment for their wares. Now, if a Jesuit receives or collects some of the furs, to help pay the enormous expenses that have to be incurred in Missions so distant, to win these people to Jesus Christ and restore peace among them, it would be desirable that those very persons who ought to incur these expenses for the preservation of the country should, at least, not be the first to condemn the zeal of those Fathers, and in their tales to paint them blacker than their gowns. They write to us from France that they can no longer provide means for the heavy expenditure that we incur in these new undertakings. We devote to them our labours, our sweat, our blood and our lives."

In cases of crime the punishment, whether of white or red men, was invariably a fine payable in beaver skins. Even murder was pardoned with such payment. In one case a whole Huron village was called to account for murder and was compelled to pay the injured tribe " as many as sixty presents the least of which must be of the value of a new beaver robe."

Everything was valued by the standard of beaver skins. The profits resulting from the monopoly of the trade must have been enormous. One of the Jesuits in writing to a brother priest in 1638 says, " Our plates although of wood cost more than yours for they are valued at one beaver robe, which is a hundred francs." Yet the Indians thought themselves well paid for the skins they brought as will be seen by their saying, "The beaver does everything perfectly well, it makes kettles, hatchets, swords, knives, bread; and in short makes everything. The English (probably meaning the white people) have no sense; they give us twenty knives like this for one beaver skin." And the Indian (in 1657) was willing to pay one winter beaver skin for two pots of wine. As far back as 1647, the Tadousac trade, which was chiefly beaver skins, amounted to 40,000 livres profit, and in all to about 250,000 livres, and two years earlier 20,000 pounds of skins were carried away in two vessels. Internal warfare both between the various tribes of Indians and between them and the whites had a marked effect on the number of skins taken each year. In 1653, before the devastation of the

Huron, it was said that " a hundred canoes used to come to trade, all laden with beaver skins and each year we had two or three hundred thousand livres worth. That was a fine revenue with which to satisfy all the people and defray the heavy expenses of the country," and this in spite of the fact that the Iroquois did all they could to prevent the trade by incessant attacks on all who either trapped or carried the skins. In the above-mentioned year there is the following statement : " The country is not stripped of beaver ; they form its gold mines and its wealth, which have only to be drawn upon in the lakes and streams, where the supply is great in proportion to the smallness of the draught upon it during these latter years due to the fear of being dispersed or captured by the Iroquois." During the earlier years, the whites contented themselves with trading for skins, but gradually the desire for greater profits led them to indulge in trapping, and in 1656 I find almost the first notice of this in the following : " As nothing happened all winter long to mar our joy and as the atmosphere of peace had spread throughout the country especially in Montreal, the great number of beaver inhabiting the streams and neighbouring rivers attracted our Frenchmen thither as spring opened and the snow and ice melted. On all sides they hunted and waged war against these animals in good earnest, with pleasure and profit alike. A young surgeon in pursuit of his prey—laying his snares for the beaver in remote places where never had solitude seemed to him sweeter—a band of Onneiochronnon Iroquois, who had gone thither to hunt men, captured this hunter of animals." This led to much trouble which fortunately did not end in bloodshed, as by diplomacy and the fairness of a chief of the Onnontachronon Iroquois named Sagochiendagnté, and the surgeon, after being badly frightened, returned to Montreal.

It is curious that while the Indians killed and eat the beaver, esteeming it the greatest luxury of the country, that they should regard the animal as being in some senses sacred to such an extent that under no conditions might the bones be given to their dogs, but gathered with the utmost care and put into the pond for fear that the beaver spirit should be offended. So great was their solicitude for the proper treatment of the animals' bones that even when they gave a beaver as a present, Father Le Jeune says, it was accompanied by the request that the recipient "should be most careful not to give the bones to the dogs, otherwise they believe they will take no more beavers." When it was not convenient to put the remains in a pond or river, they burned them to avoid any possibility of their hunting being spoiled.

Needless to say the pursuit of the beaver led to bloodshed in many instances, for not only did individuals commit murders, but tribal wars resulted in which horrible atrocities were committed. The white traders, in their eagerness to procure the skins from the Indians, supplied them with arms which were far more deadly than the primitive bows and arrows, with the inevitable result of increasing the casualties in the wars, and as one tribe was often more favoured than another in the way of arms, the ill feeling between them was fostered to a terrible extent. In 1659 the Dutch traders supplied the Algonquins with fire-arms, and this led to the practical annihilation of the Agnieronnons and others. But their triumph was not long-lived, for in the following year there is a statement that " the skin of the latter (beaver) is of so little value to them (the Algonquins), since the Iroquois has prevented its sale that they broil the beaver over the fire as is done with swine in France."

At this time the Algonquins settled in the Hudson Bay region, driven there apparently by the unceasing attacks made upon them by the Iroquois. So the beaver was to the Indian what gold has so often been to the white man—a rich gift of nature converted into a cause of bloodshed. Not only did this apply to the Indians, but through the jealousies of the rival trading companies the enmity of the tribes was incited against their rivals with terribly disastrous results. Still further was bloodshed caused by the innocent beaver, for the vessels carrying the valuable cargoes of furs from Canada were regarded as treasure ships, and we find mention of French vessels "richly laden with the spoils of the beaver of this country" being captured by "the English, who were waiting for it in the Channel."

From the very beginning the fur trade was stained with blood, and yet perhaps it might be said that the blood was shed for the good of the country. "The richly furred and highly prized skins formed the chief staple of Canadian commerce." They paid its debts. Men grew rich on them. Vast fortunes such as the Astors' were founded almost entirely on beaver skins. The Hudson Bay Company, one of the most powerful and successful companies that the world has ever known, owed its existence to furs, the most important being the beaver. This company was largely responsible for the opening up of Canada, the search for the skins taking their factors into even the most remote parts; in other words, civilisation—in a modified form perhaps—was carried into the wilderness in exchange for beaver pelts. In times of distress caused by famine or illness this great company rendered assistance to the improvident Indians, giving them food, medicine and clothing in exchange for their word that the results of the trapping should be taken by the Hudson Bay Company. Whether abuses ever crept into the management of the outlying districts I cannot say, but certainly on the whole their affairs were well conducted for the benefit of the Indian on whose welfare the Company so largely depended. Notwithstanding what has been said to the contrary the use of " fire-water " was certainly discountenanced. This in itself was a potent cause of peace. There is no doubt that many serious wars were averted by the diplomatic handling of what were often extremely difficult situations. (This is not a book on Canada, so that I scarcely feel justified in going too much into historical questions, but if the reader is interested in the subject he will find great pleasure in going through the accounts of the Hudson Bay Company, " The Relations of the Jesuits in Canada," and other historic works relating to the subject.)

As already stated the coin of the country was the beaver-skin ; it was the unit of exchange or barter. If a man wanted a blanket or a knife or any article he was asked so many " beaver," and though he did not always pay in actual skins they were the basis of all smaller transactions. Unfortunately it is impossible to estimate the number of beaver which were killed for use and sale. In 1854 no less than 509,000 skins were sold in London and Edinburgh, while Thompson Seton gives the average annual total " brought out by the American Fur Company and the Hudson's Bay Company for the period between 1860 and 1870, when the fur trade was at its height, as, in round numbers, 150,000," and he adds : " But the

natives used as many good pelts as they sold and
seldom saved the skins of those taken in summer,
though they killed for food the whole year round,
so that 500,000 per annum is more likely to represent the aggregate destruction by man." How
nearly correct this is it is impossible to say, but
we do know that whatever the number that have
been killed each year it has nearly always been
greater than it should have been, a statement
easily proved by the rapid disappearance of the
animals throughout the greater part of their range.

The following account written by Mr. R. Mac-
Farlane, who was chief factor of the Hudson's Bay
Company, and published by the Smithsonian
Institution (Washington) gives some interesting
facts and figures : " If let alone, or not much
disturbed by hunting, the beaver will rapidly
increase in numbers. In proof of this statement, I
would mention that many extensive tracts of
country in which they had become scarce or had
wholly or almost entirely disappeared (as a result
of the keen and very costly rivalry in trade which
had for many years existed between the Northwest
Company of Montreal and the Hudson's Bay Company of England previous to their coalition in 1821,
it was uncertain for some time ' which of them
lost most money—neither of them gained money,'
while the general demoralization of Indians and
whites was very lamentable) they afterwards recovered under the fostering policy of protection

promptly inaugurated and intelligently pursued by the now united Fur Trading and Governing Corporation. For more than a decade subsequent to 1821 each beaver district in the chartered and licensed territories of the Hudson's Bay Company was annually restricted to the collection of a certain fixed number of beaver, which course eventually proved of much benefit to all concerned. By this means the perpetuation of the beaver was insured in sections where reckless slaughter had almost exterminated it, while the resulting expansion in more forward localities naturally followed. With the view, however, of reconciling them to this enforced mode of preservation, the natives were strongly urged and encouraged to devote their best energies to the trapping of martens and other fur-bearing animals. After the beaver were known to have largely increased in numbers, and still sold well, the above rule was gradually relaxed ; and as the wants of the Indians in those days were comparatively few, they never experienced any particular hardship from the limit thus imposed upon them in the general interest. It may be here mentioned that the Company never encouraged the hunting of beaver or any other pelt *out of season*. On the contrary they strictly prohibited the killing of beaver in summer, and would only reluctantly accept the skins of such animals as they were assured had been absolutely necessary for food purposes.

" The introduction of nutria and silk in the manufacture of hats in the early forties of the last century struck a deadly blow at the value of beaver, the chief staple fur of Canada and the north-west for two centuries, from which it has not yet quite recovered. For nearly half a century thereafter, the prices annually obtained for pelts were some 60 and 70 per cent. below the average which had previously ruled. Since the Alaska fur seal, however, has come into 'fashion' very much better rates have been realised by the smaller quantities of beaver sold in recent years. With the view of obtaining better prices in England, as well as for its future increase in numbers, the Company naturally favoured a continuation of its beneficial policy of restriction ; but owing to the then general abundance of beaver, and the advent of competition in the trade, this much desired course had to be gradually abandoned. For the twenty-five years, from 1853 to 1877, the Hudson's Bay Company sold a total of nearly three million skins (2,965,389) of this important animal in the world's fur mart— London. The yearly catch from 1853, with 55,456 pelts, to 87,013 in 1858 exhibited a steady increase. The year 1859, with 107,196 pelts, was, I believe, the first to reach and exceed the century mark since the union in 1821, but 1860 dropped to 91,459. While 1861 was only 926 skins below 1859, 1862 produced 115,580 pelts, 1863 produced 114,149, and 1864 produced 142,998, yet the last-

Beavers gathering their supply of wood. (*Painting.*)

Beavers working on their dam. (*Painting.*)

mentioned year's sale was immediately followed by a decline of 24,750 pelts. The balance of the series from 1866 to 1877 varies between the minimum, 115,646 in 1877, and the maximum, 172,042 in 1867, certainly the highest and best since 1821, and probably one of, if not the most productive in the history of the Hudson's Bay Company. An old writer of repute, however, writes that 175,000 beaver skins were collected by the 'ancient concern' in one year about the middle of the eighteenth century. It is possible that this large number may have comprised the country trade of two seasons. European wars were rather frequent and somewhat protracted in those days, while it is on record that one or two of the Company's ships failed in making the annual round voyage between London and Hudson Bay. I think it is a matter of regret that neither of the two recent historians of the Hudson's Bay Company, while throwing much light on the earlier and some of their later trade operations, have not also given us some definite statements of their yearly fur shipments and sales, which would have been generally appreciated. Mr. Beckles Willson has, however, given an interesting account of the Company's first London public sale, which took place on January 24, 1672. On this occasion the 3,000 weight of beaver were put up in thirty lots, and fetched from 36 to 55 shillings (a pound probably). The other furs and peltries, bear, marten, and otter, &c., were reserved for a separate

and subsequent auction, while previous receipts
from the Bay had been disposed of by private
treaty.

"This first official sale, as it subsequently proved,
of a series of great transactions which for upward
of two centuries have made London the centre of
the world's fur trade, excited the greatest interest,
and both the Prince of Wales and the Duke of
York, besides Dryden, the poet, were among the
many spectators. Previous to the advent of
Canadian traders from the East, the Indians of the
surrounding country were wont to assemble in the
spring at Lake Winnipeg to the number of perhaps
1,500, where also birch-bark canoes were built. Six
hundred of these containing a thousand hunters,
exclusive of women, came down annually to York
factory with furs to trade. Beaver were very
numerous in those days, and a great many were
wasted in various ways, often as clothing and
bedding. Not a few were hung on trees as native
offerings upon the death of a child or near relation ;
occasionally the fur was burned off, and the beaver
roasted whole for food banquets among the Indians.

"He further states that in 1742, two large expeditions of natives from the interior came down to
York and Churchill (Fort Prince of Wales). One
of them had 200 packs of 100 skins each (20,000
beaver, probably from Lake Winnipeg country),
and the other 300 packs of 100 each (30,000
beaver and 9,000 martens). This made a total of

50,000 beaver received from both 'expeditions.' I take it that these came from the Chipewyan Indians of the distant Athabasca and intervening country, reaching Churchill by way of the English and Churchill rivers.

" Doctor Bryce, in his concise history, writes that so effective and successful were the operations of the Great Northwest Company of Montreal, that toward the end of the eighteenth century a single year's trade produce was enormous, and comprised 106,000 beaver, 32,000 martens, 11,800 minks, 10,000 musquash, and 17,000 skins of other animals. Still, if we knew the total Hudson's Bay Company's catch for that year, I doubt if both returns of beaver would much exceed the total of 172,042 skins given in the London fur sale statement for 1867. From 1858 to 1884 the district of Athabasca contributed 445,014, or an average of 17,116 a year, to the Company's London sales. The average for the self-same posts for the five outfits (1885 to 1889) is about 8,000 ; and with the ' opposition ' trade added from 1890 to the spring of 1903, both will undoubtedly exhibit a further decline. From 1863 to 1883 Mackenzie River District exported a total of 183,216 beaver, giving an average of 11,822 a year. For the three years (1886, 1887, 1889) of which I hold data, it had fallen to 6,852, and is, I fear, very much lower at the present time. These are but samples of the general decrease in beaver receipts experienced at every trade competing point from Quebec to the North Pacific and from the international boundary to Hudson's Bay and the north-western limit of its range in arctic America.

" It is now well-known that for some years prior to the coalition in 1821, the annual catch of beaver was rapidly dwindling, and that in several sections it had been exterminated by reckless slaughter ; another decade or two of similar trade competition would doubtless have led to its extinction, except for a time in retreats remote and difficult of access. We have had ample proof, however, by obtained results, of the beneficial operation of the wise and far-reaching policy adopted by Governor Sir George Simpson and the able and experienced fur-trade counsellors of the then united companies, for the due preservation of this valuable animal. For some years before and after the transfer of the country to Canada in 1870, the entire Peace River, together with many other streams and small ponds throughout the Territories, British Columbia, the Yukon, and the east were swarming with beaver ; but this, unfortunately, is not the case to-day. From 1853 to 1877 inclusive, the average number of skins sold by the Hudson's Bay Company in London was 118,615, as against their total catalogue sales of about 50,000 for 1897, 43,000 in 1900, 46,000 in 1902, and 49,190 for 1903. This is, without doubt, a bad showing for some of the later of the twenty-six years which have succeeded that statement.

Even with the addition thereto of the 'opposition' trade, in the very same locality, it is doubtful if the aggregate of both would greatly exceed one-half of this average. It is generally assumed that 'opposition' or competition is the 'life of trade' in all branches of business; but in the opinion of many competent judges, the fur trade, from its very nature and the scope of its operations, is, or should be, one of the few essential exceptions to the rule. It is a matter of fact that the advent and continued presence of 'free traders' at a Company's inland post has always had a more or less stimulating effect on the natives by inducing them to exert themselves to a larger degree than usual in the hunting of beaver and all other fur-bearing animals, but although at first and for some time all concerned appear to benefit by increased returns, yet the inevitable accompaniment of reckless and indiscriminate slaughter, sooner or later, adversely manifests itself. This has hitherto been the invariable experience at every assailed post or district in North America.

"We all know how the bison or buffalo of the prairies of Canada and the United States has practically disappeared, although half a century ago it was reckoned by millions. The beaver has been Canada's staple fur for centuries, and but for the Hudson's Bay Company and its officers it would long ago have ceased to exist as a commercial asset. Unless further action speedily intervenes in the

premises, however, the ultimate extermination of
the Canadian beaver is merely a question of time.
It has already disappeared for good from many
sections in which it was formerly present. It is
becoming very scarce in certain localities where it
should receive immediate protection in the way of
several legally-assured years of rest and full exemp-
tion from disturbance by hunters. In other
districts, where it is generally but surely diminishing in numbers, its killing should be restricted on
lines similar to those pursued by the Company for
many years subsequent to 1821. Greater latitude
might be accorded to hunting in now unknown and
not easily accessible parts where it probably
abounds ; but except for food absolutely required
no one should be permitted to trap or shoot beaver
out of season. It is useless making rules and regulations, however, unless they be strictly enforced.
The woodland buffalo is now receiving some well-
deserved attention in this regard, and it is about
time that the musk ox should be protected from
indiscriminate slaughter solely for the sake of his
head or hide : there should be a seasonable limit
imposed upon hunters thereof. Neither should the
mountain goat and sheep, the elk, and the valuable
food animals—the moose and woodland caribou—
be neglected in this connection. And although the
Barren Ground reindeer is still abundant, yet the
northern Indian should not be permitted to continue or resume their ancient vicious course of reck-

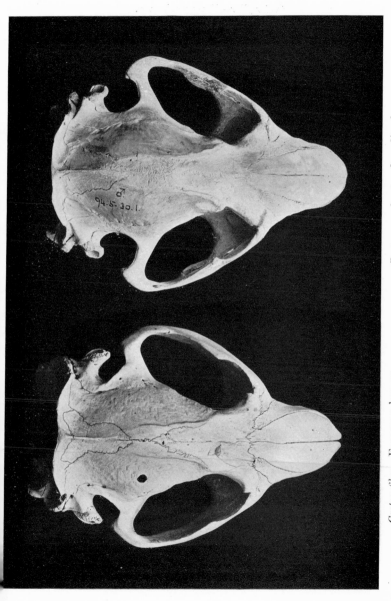

Castor fiber—European beaver.   *Castor canadensis*—Canadian beaver.

(From Museum of Natural History, South Kensington.)

Castor fiber—European beaver.
(From Museum of Natural History, South Kensington.)

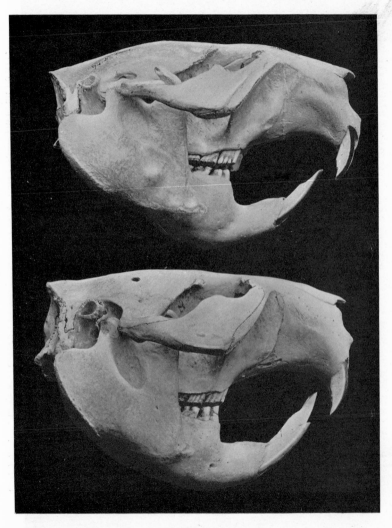

Castor canadensis—Canadian beaver.
(From Museum of Natural History, South Kensington.)

less and indiscriminate slaughter of them whenever the opportunity appeared."

In former times when the Indians had the almost exclusive trapping they were systematic in their work, and the number taken from each colony was seldom in excess of what would keep the numbers fairly stationary. When the white man entered the competition his one idea was to secure the

Label of the Hudson's Bay Company, as used at the present time.

largest possible crop of skins, utterly regardless of whether or not he killed the goose that laid the golden egg. The result was inevitable and the wasteful destruction reduced the crop to such a low level that from the animals' entire range probably not more than 30,000 skins have been taken in any one year for some time past. At one time it was quite a question whether the beaver was not on the very verge of extermination. The passing of protective laws and the making of parks or reserves have, we hope, rendered this fear groundless, and the beaver that has done so much in the past to help in the development of Canada will find sanctuary in the land of its forefathers. So that the prediction made by Lydekker in 1894 in which he says "both the European and American beaver are doomed to extinction as wild animals at no very distant date" will not be fulfilled.

CHAPTER V

THE BEAVER AS A SPECIES

Castor canadensis and Castor fiber.

OF the order rodentia the beaver is the second in point of size, the only species exceeding it being the Capibara (Hydrochoerus capivars) of South America. The American and European beaver constitute the only living representatives of the genus castor, and the difference between the two is so very slight as to be scarcely noticeable to any-one but a scientist. Externally, except in point of size, the two species are practically identical, the American being slightly larger, but an examination of the skulls shows certain minor differences, chief of which is the slightly greater proportional length of the nasal bones and narrower skull of the European species (Castor fiber). Another less noticeable mark of distinction is that the castoreum obtained from the European species, especially those from Russia, is more valuable and contains a greater proportion of castorin resin and albumen. In point of age the beaver is evidently an animal of great antiquity, not only in its present form but the larger and extinct Trogontherium (of Europe) and the Castoroides (of America), neither of which are believed to be the ancestors of the present-day species, as their fossilised remains have been found in the pliocene deposits in which were preserved the skeletons of the Mastodon and Mammoth, so that these animals lived during the tertiary period and from the evidence which nature thus preserved there is no reason to believe that the beaver, as we know them to-day, differs in any marked way from those of prehistoric ages. The earliest European Beaver was probably the *chalicomys* which has been found in the Miocene beds of the Continent. It was considerably smaller than the existing form and " differed from all living rodents in having a perforation of the lower end of the upper arm-bone or humerus " (Lydekker). The largest of the family was the Castoroides, whose skull was only about four inches less in length than that of a lion and was probably the largest of any of the rodents. The beaver, both American and European, had the largest range of any animal, those in Europe having existed all over Europe, including Great Britain (not Ireland) and Asia as far as the Euphrates. During the Pleistocene period they lived in Italy as far as Rome, while the American species ranged all over North America from the Arctic Sea to Mexico. At the present time the American beaver, *Castor Canadensis*, is chiefly restricted to the more northern portion of the Continent of North America ; none are found in the region of the great plains, nor in the more southerly and easterly

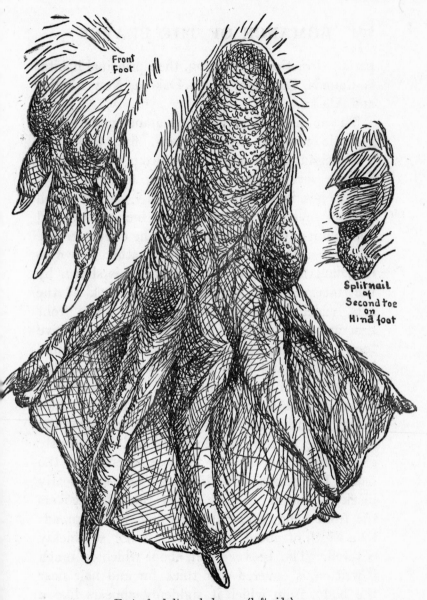

Front
Foot

Splitnail
of
Second toe
on
Hind foot

Feet of adult male beaver (left side).

(After drawing by Ernest Thompson Seton (from "Life Histories of Northern
Animals").)

parts.   Practically speaking, their principal habitat is Canada, Colorado, South Dakota, New Mexico and Alaska.

The animal is in general appearance much like a gigantic muskrat with a broad, flat, thick tail. The weight of an adult ranges from thirty-five to sixty or seventy pounds, length up to about forty-five inches, including tail, the scaly part of which is from seven to nine-and-a-half inches long and approximately half that width.   The circumference of the body at its largest part is rather over two feet, and the heaviness of the build is shown by the measurement around the neck back of the ears, which is about fourteen inches.   The front legs are very short with small feet having five toes.   The hind legs are also short but much more heavily built and have the feet webbed from the base of each of the five toe-nails.   All toes are furnished with strong nails, those of the front foot being slightly narrower and longer.   On the second toe of the hind foot the nail is curiously cleft, presumably for the purpose of combing the hair.   The palms of both feet are bare and nearly black in colour.   A soft, rather thick hair covers the front hand, while the hind foot, which spreads to a width of about nine inches, is not so thickly covered.   The beaver's tail, about which so much is written, is covered with thick fur and hair near the body, from which it suddenly appears like a broad paddle completely covered with a hard, scaly

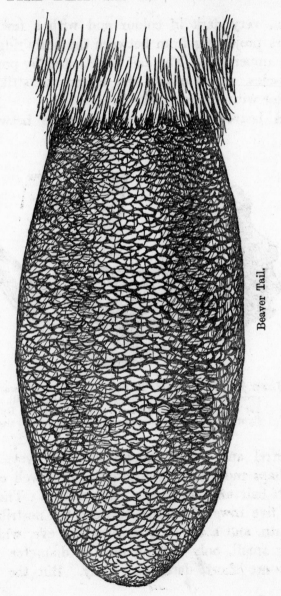

Beaver Tail.

R.B.   P

skin, very dark in colour and with a few short hairs projecting from between the scaly ridges on the upper side. The tail is actuated by powerful muscles, which enable the animal to strike the water with extraordinary force.

A beaver's head resembles a cross between a

Lower jaw of beaver with the near side of jaw cut away in order to show the total length of the incisor tooth and the comparatively small amount that projects. Upper figures are the molars or grinding teeth (⅞ natural size).

squirrel and a rat, though in some ways it is perhaps more like a guinea-pig. It is well coated with hair and fur except the nostrils. The face has five rows of bristles between the nostrils and mouth, and a few bristles over the eye, which is very small, only half an inch in diameter. The ears are short, dark, and hairy. But the most peculiar feature of the head are the teeth, which are most wonderfully developed to meet the animal's method of living. Their total number is twenty, ten in each jaw. These consist of eight molars or grinding teeth and two incisors for cutting. These latter are the chisel-like teeth with which the beaver is able to cut down the great forest trees. In their construction they are of especial interest. The outside or front is a thin layer of very hard orange-coloured enamel attached

Skeleton of Beaver.

to a thick backing of dentine, which, being soft, wears away by the action of cutting and leaves the shell-like edge of enamel always sharp. The lower teeth are of great length, approximately four inches along the outer curve, of which a minimum of about one quarter extends beyond the jaw-bone. The incisors of the upper jaw are both shorter and more abruptly curved. The distance between these and the molars is about one-and-a-half times the space occupied by the groups of molars. These are curious rootless teeth composed of foliated hard enamel, the inside of the folds being filled with soft dentine, which wears away and leaves the ridges sharp and capable of grinding wood or bark to a fine pulp. All the teeth grow continually to make up for the natural wear. In case a tooth is injured or broken the opposite one grows to abnormal length, frequently to the great discomfiture of the animal. The folds of hard enamel continue with little change of form down to the base of the teeth, but the semi-hard dentine is only formed near the grinding surface. The young beaver is born with well-developed teeth, which differ only in point of size from those of the adult.

The brain of the beaver is noticeably smooth and lacking in the corrugations which are supposed to indicate intelligence. It seems peculiar that an animal which has so much (from our standard of comparison) to signify inferiority should, by its works, prove itself to be so highly intelligent. Romanes says: "There is no animal—not even excepting the ants and bees—whose instinct has risen to a higher level of far-reaching adaptation to certain constant conditions of environment, or whose faculties, undoubtedly instinctive, are more puzzlingly wrought up with faculties no less undoubtedly intelligent."

The beaver's coat is composed, like that of nearly all fur-bearing animals, of fur and hair. In the beaver it is thick, woolly, brown fur about

Le Beau's marvellous vision, published in 1738. It is interesting to note the six beavers engaged in cutting down a tree, also the well-made hurdles on the dam.

In birch bark canoes like this the beaver skins were carried from the wilds to Montreal and other centres.

three-quarters of an inch in length, while the hair is from two to two-and-a-half inches long, dark in colour and fairly shiny. The general colour of the animal is chestnut brown, but it varies considerably according to locality, from a lightish yellow to very dark brown, and in very rare instances to almost black. Albinism, either partial or complete, is comparatively rare. The colour of the young beaver is decidedly greyer than that of the adults, the length of one four days old is about fourteen inches.

Outwardly there is nothing to distinguish the sexes, except when the female is suckling her young; then her four teats, which are situated between the fore legs, are slightly enlarged. The number of young at birth varies from two to six, rarely more, the common number being four. They are born between the end of April and beginning of June after a period of gestation which is believed to last about fourteen weeks.

In swimming the beaver uses its hind legs and to a very limited extent its tail, chiefly for sudden starts and turns. In this respect it differs entirely from the muskrat, which swims chiefly with its tail, which acts as a scull. The front feet are, as the trappers say, " put into its waistcoat pockets," in other words, held downwards along the sides. The head is clearly visible when the animal swims and the top of the back more or less so according to the speed at which it is going. When lying perfectly still at the surface of the water the tail also may be seen.   Under water the head is held lower or more directly in line with the body as far as I have been able to judge, and they can remain under water for six or seven minutes or even more, according to some observers.   When submerged the ears are closed, as also are the nostrils, except when slightly opened to emit the vitiated air.

In slapping the water with the tail it has been fairly well proved by means of my photographs that the position assumed by the animal is not at all according to previously published accounts in which the impression has been given that the head is down or even under water at the moment of the slap, whereas the head and the shoulders are actually held very high out of the water as the tail is raised.   The action is so rapid that it is practically indistinguishable to the eye.   In diving the beaver can go down so quietly that there is no disturbance to the water's surface.

On land the beaver walks with its back much arched and tail dragging ; when listening it usually stands erect on its hind feet with the tail used as a balance, and when sitting down it often brings the tail round forward and even sits on it, though personally I have never seen this position.   The eyesight of the beaver is fairly keen, but they depend more on their extremely acute senses of hearing and smell, particularly the latter, which is very highly developed.   Like most wild animals they realise the importance of wind and always select the lee side of a pond when on watch.

Castoreum, for which the beaver is famous and has been for at least twenty-four hundred years, is a peculiar substance secreted in two glands situated below the pubis. It has a mild and not unpleasant odour which is supposed to be very attractive to many kinds of animals and consequently is used by nearly all trappers in preparing "medicine" with which to lure the various fur-bearers to the traps. It is also believed to possess extraordinary medicinal properties, and has been in use for over two thousand years. Martin states that "the earliest references we have to the beaver in history date back to 500 B.C., when Hippocrates mentioned it in connection with medicinal uses of castoreum, and from the fact that Pliny wrote that the creature's life was spared on surrender of the valuable pouches of castoreum, we gather that it was for these alone that the animal was hunted." The substance in various forms was used as a cure for headaches, deafness, abscesses, gout, epilepsy, colic, toothache, sciatica, lethargy, fever, pleurisy, "induces sleep and prevents sleepiness," helps memory and cures tuberculosis and rheumatism, and is of benefit to mad people. It was also used in smoking with soothing effect by the Indians. Surely an array of virtues not surpassed by even the most imaginative quack doctors in advertising their "cure-alls!" We may laugh at the ancients for their faith in castoreum, but they were not altogether alone in their belief, for it is to-day highly prized if we may judge from the fact that it is sold for about ten dollars per pound. It takes the " castors " of four or five or even six beavers to yield a pound of the substance and the demand always, I am told, exceeds the supply. From this we must believe that we do not differ very much from the ancients.

Besides the castoreum the beaver fat also was considered valuable for medicinal purposes by the Indians who used it, among other things, for preventing and curing frost-bite and for rubbing limbs afflicted with rheumatism just as some of the African tribes use the lion's fat. Beaver teeth were employed to some extent by Indians as chisels before they learned the value of metal.

But perhaps the greatest commercial value of the beaver was the fur which was used for making hats. During the seventeenth and eighteenth centuries the beaver hat was of even greater importance than the silk hat is to-day, and very much more expensive, for the price of a good "beaver" ranged as high as eighty or ninety shillings, and, strange to say, old skins that had been in use were more sought after than new ones. Later on other furs were used for making hatter's felt ; this reduced the demand for the beaver skins, while the discovery of silk plush, as a substitute material for hats, practically ended the use of beaver fur so far as the hatter was concerned. Now its furs are only used for the adornment of people, as linings of coats, collars, and muffs, and other similar purposes. They are made up either with the hair on or plucked so that the thick fur alone remains.

The Canadian beaver is divided into five more or less distinct races, which are given by E. T. Seton as—

Castor canadensis, Kuhl, the typical form and smallest (a).

Castor carolinensis, Rhoads, larger than the type with broader tail (b).

Castor frondator, Mearns, larger and paler than the type, with scaly part of tail shorter than twice the width (c).

Castor pacificus, Rhoads, largest and darkest of all, with scaly part of tail longer than twice the width (d).

Castor texensis, Bailey, very large and pale, with scaly part of tail longer than twice the width.

The distribution of the type, *Castor canadensis*, is approximately the whole of Canada, and northern United States to within three or four hundred miles of the Pacific Coast, and down to about latitude 38 degrees, except in the part west of longitude 103 degrees, where *frondator* is found. In the central southern portion of the United States they are classed as *texensis*, while those in the south-eastern states are *carolinensis* and all that are found on the Pacific coast are called *Castor pacificus.*

The European beaver, *Castor fiber*, still exists in a few places in Europe, chiefly, I believe, in Norway, where, in 1883, there were said to be about one hundred near Arendal ; these have been strictly protected and have therefore increased. Formerly they existed in great numbers throughout most parts of Europe, also in Asia, northern and central. In Livonia as recently as 1724 they were so abundant that they were considered a nuisance and the last is said to have been killed in 1841. In Holland they were exterminated in 1825, while in western Germany the Moselle and the Maas were noted for the number of beaver. In 1829 there was a flourishing colony on the Elbe near Magdeburg.

In England and Wales the beaver was found up to about the twelfth century ; the Welsh name was Llost-Llydden, signifying broad-tail. The last record of them in that country was, according to Giraldus Cambrensis, in 1188, when they were found in the Teivy, Cardiganshire. King Howel Dda, who died in 948, fixed the price of beaver skins at 120 pence, which shows how greatly they were appreciated, as fox, wolf and stag were valued at only eight pence. The beaver's name in England has been perpetuated by very few places such as Beaverage, Beverley, Beversbrook and Beaverbourne, in marked contrast to the United States and Canada where the name will be preserved by literally thousands of towns, villages, rivers, streams, lakes and ponds. In Scotland the beaver continued later than in England, but curiously enough there is nothing to show that it has ever existed in Ireland.

HINTS ON BEAVER PHOTOGRAPHY.

FEW animals large or small are less suited to photography than the beaver. To begin, they are rather shapeless, with inconspicuous legs, no pattern in the way of colouring, and what makes the work doubly difficult and unsatisfactory is that they are so seldom to be seen by daylight. Add to this the fact that they are usually wet and very shy, and it will be easily understood that the task of securing really good photographs is not easy. I may even say that in all my experience of hunting with the camera no animals have ever given me so much trouble. The best pictures I have ever obtained of lions and other big and dangerous beasts were secured with far less difficulty than even the worst of my beaver studies. This is said so that those who may attempt the work will not be disappointed if success is slow in coming. The surest way is of course by flashlight and the surest place is at the dam. A small break in the structure will be almost certain to induce the beaver to come to repair it, as they don't like to let the water escape.

The camera may be placed on or near the dam so that the opening is about in the centre of the plate. A black thread across the breach, about five inches above water-level (to avoid muskrats), attached to the flashlight and shutter should answer the purpose if you have a satisfactory outfit, but bear in mind that every part of the apparatus must be protected from damp, and sufficiently firmly placed to prevent being blown over by sudden winds. It is not necessary as a rule to conceal the camera, as the beaver pays but little attention to it ; he is more interested in the scent left by man, so it is as well to throw water over footprints and anything near the ground that has been handled. If all goes well you will get lots of exposures, but in most cases the pictures will show simply a shapeless mass of wet fur to take the place of the beaver. Such at least has been my experience, for out of about thirty exposures only four or five showed the animal with any shape. Don't forget that the beaver moves quickly, so the exposure should be very short. On land the difficulties increase enormously. There are so many trees to which the animal *may* come that it is no easy task to select the one to which he *will* come. The surest way is to lay a seductive branch of birch or maple on a regular pathway, and arrange the camera accordingly. When work is being done on the lodges there is always a chance of securing photographs of the animal carrying up mud or sticks, but great precaution must be taken not to disturb the surroundings, or cause suspicions, and everything should be done as quietly as possible. Be sure not to let moisture condense on the lens of your camera. This causes more failures than anyone will believe. During the autumn in northern countries everything becomes covered with a fine mist-like condensation. This is particularly noticeable on glass, and you cannot get a sharp image through it. Therefore wipe the lens thoroughly or protect it carefully by means of a hood which will open immediately before the exposure. I dare not give information as to the best kind of outfit to use, for I have not yet found such a thing. Some new devices are being offered now, but not having tried them I do not feel justified in either giving their names or in recommending them. So far I have had the best results with electric apparatus, as they are quick, almost silent and fairly convenient, but they don't always work. If using any sort of electric device, be sure to have an ample supply of batteries to take the place of those that through mishap become exhausted. I have had a tree dropped on my outfit, branches pulled between the legs of the tripod, which was of course upset, and many other accidents, which go to show that the pitfalls of beaver photography are many and trying. A good temper, plenty of patience, a reasonably good outfit and a proper share of luck are the ingredients necessary. All successful photographs will be well earned, and consequently they will be greatly appreciated, at least by him who has the good fortune to make them. To avoid too much disappointment it is just as well to develop all flashlight exposures *before* resetting the cameras, as the number of ways in which failure may come is limitless.

INDEX

BRADBURY, AGNEW, & CO. LD., PRINTERS, LONDON AND TONBRIDGE.